LIVING ON HOPE WHILE LIVING IN BABYLON

Living on Hope While Living in Babylon

The Christian Anarchists of the Twentieth Century

TRIPP YORK

WIPF & STOCK · Eugene, Oregon

LIVING ON HOPE WHILE LIVING IN BABYLON
The Christian Anarchists of the Twentieth Century

Wipf & Stock
A Division of Wipf and Stock Publishers
199 W. 8th Ave., Suite 3
Eugene, OR 97401

www.wipfandstock.com

ISBN 13: 978-1-55635-685-8

Manufactured in the U.S.A.

To my grandfather, Ewell Joe Seay (1910–1993):
Though he never listened to The Clash, he understood
what it meant to "step lightly" and "stay free."

Behold, with what companions I walked the streets
of Babylon and wallowed in its mire . . .
—St. Augustine

Contents

Acknowledgments ix

Introduction xi

1   A Christian Anarchist Politic 1

2   Apocalyptic Politics 17

3   Catholic Workers Unite! 37

4   Clarence Jordan's Fellowship 60

5   The Brothers Berrigan 81

    Epilogue: Failing Faithfully 103

    Bibliography 111

    Index 115

Acknowledgments

This book began as a master's thesis while I was studying at Duke Divinity School, though its origins can be traced to a much earlier period. In high school, I began reading a number of Russian and Spanish anarchists. They were not introduced to me by my teachers, but by the subculture associated with 1980s punk rock and hard-core. Bands such as Oi Polloi, Crass, and the Dead Kennedys, while antithetical to the theological claims of my tradition, taught me to pay careful attention to the ways we are shaped and formed by those in power—including ecclesial power. I eventually discovered even more intellectually satisfying bands such as Bad Religion, Propagandhi, and boysetsfire, all who, in a very Foucaultian manner, not only questioned the acceptance of norms, but challenged the linguistic paradigms that render the word "norm" comprehensible. Listening to, and learning from, these musical anti-structuralists remain, for me, far more edifying than reading either Chomsky or Derrida.

I admit that much of my early fascination with anarchism was juvenile and motivated by little more than a desire to resist authority. As Stephen R. L. Clark suggests, if anarchism is simply an antipathy towards authority, then all of us, since modernity, are anarchists. I quickly learned that anarchy is not simply the spray painting of graffiti on walls or on the bottom of our $150 skateboards, but a different way of being in the world. This "difference" is what I found to be most attractive about it. Unfortunately, anarchism is embedded within modern discourse, and though it offers an alternative to the left and the right, it nevertheless remains entrenched in the discourse that renders both the left and the right intelligible. It is simply not different enough.

By the time of this realization I was studying for my master's degree at Duke when I was introduced to the lives of Catholic anarchists, excommunicated Southern Baptists, and the Anabaptists. It was during my time at Duke that the possibility of anarchistic Christianity started making sense. This is not because anyone there considers themselves anarchists, but because they are so concerned with what it means to faithfully embody Christian discipleship. I, therefore, owe a special thanks to Joel Shuman, William Willimon, and Amy Laura Hall for nurturing me in my pursuit of what it means to take seriously the dissident path of Jesus. I owe a special debt of gratitude to my thesis advisor Stanley Hauerwas, who provided, on my thesis, a number of helpful criticisms (riddled with expletives) which forced me to better articulate my arguments. Stanley loves to show his endorsement of Christian anarchy by reminding us that "children are proof that God is an anarchist!" Though he humorously attributes a chaotic element inherent within anarchism, the idea that Christians must live lives out of control seems correct. To relinquish control, to give up the pursuit of power over history, governments, and especially theology may be the most daunting task of those who would follow Christ.

I am now completing my fifth year of teaching at Elon University. During this time, the department has been gracious enough to allow me to take chances with a number of upper division courses, one of them entitled "Theology and Political Subversion." It was through this class that I converted my master's thesis into this book. The major change resulted in less theory and more biography. I am appreciative of the students in that course for helping me to see that the best argument one can give is one's life. I hope this book reflects such a sentiment. I am especially grateful to Jeff Pugh, head of the Religion Department at Elon, for keeping me busy these past five years. His friendship, along with my other colleagues in the department, has been immeasurable. I am also indebted to both Ginny Vellani for her careful assessment of an earlier draft of this manuscript, and to Maggie Pahos for her scrupulous work indexing this book.

This book would not have been possible if not for Charlie Collier and my editor Halden Doerge. The work that Charlie is doing with Wipf and Stock provides hope for those of us on the theological fringes of publishing. Halden's insights and criticisms were always spot-on. Any remaining mistakes are mine. Finally, I owe a special thanks to my family for their care, and, as always, to Tatiana for absolutely everything.

Tripp York
Feast of St. Blaise
Anno Domini 2009

Introduction

KINGS, IDOLS, AND DISCIPLESHIP

A short fuse to scatter steady hands if I forget to remember that better lives have been lived in the margins, locked in the prisons and lost on the gallows than have ever been enshrined in palaces.

—PROPAGANDHI (*PURINA HALL OF FAME*)

In the third chapter of the book of Daniel, we find the story of King Nebuchadnezzar's vain attempt to have all of those under his command worship his gods. The king, who only moments earlier proclaimed his undying loyalty to the God of Israel, creates a massive golden statue and demands people of every nation and tongue, at the cue of his "entire musical ensemble," to fall down and worship it. As the music played "all the peoples, nations, and languages fell down and worshipped" the golden statue (Dan 3:7).

This is not entirely true. There were a few who refused to comply. Scripture tells us there were "certain Jews . . . appointed over the affairs of the province of Babylon" who refused to obey the king. Their names were Hannaniah, Mishael, and Azaraiah, (or Shadrach, Meshach, and Abednego, as the empire sought to rename them), and their disobedience did not go unnoticed. Nebuchadnezzar was furious. He sent for the three and commanded them to immediately bow and worship his creation. If they persisted in their noncompliance, they were told they would be cast into a fiery furnace. Alas, our heroes did not relent. They refused to worship his creation. They told the king that they felt no need to make a defense for their actions, and, furthermore, if their God so chose to save them then God would do it. "But if not," they continued, "be it known to you, O King, that we will not serve your gods and we will not worship the golden statue you have set up" (Dan 3:18).

The narrative ends, as most of us are aware, with the three surviving the fire and the king going mad. It is quite the inspirational, and thus popular, story. We do so love our "tough" heroes. I fear, despite the popularity of this story (or perhaps because of it), we are tempted to domesticate and romanticize it in order for it to mesh with the kind of disembodied Christianity prevalent in North America. The first time I heard this story, for example, I could not have been much older than six, and yet it was told to me in such a way that I never got the idea that the actions of Shadrach, Meshach, and Abednego were either remotely radical or political. Of course, it may be a bit much to assume that at six years of age I should know anything more than the story itself. This may be true, but rare is the occasion that one would hear this story told in such a way that we might find *ourselves* threatened by something analogous to a furnace (a jail cell?). Despite the fact that these three men were well aware that God might not save them, they still refused to accommodate the king's wishes. Though they all worked in the service of the king, they remained capable of discerning when their leader asked that which cannot be given. I just wonder how this story could be told today so that we too could see when what is demanded of us becomes an occasion for idolatry.

Perhaps this story is much too easy. The idolatry is plain to see even by most six-year-old children. But how do we make the connection between Nebuchadnezzar's demands and the demands placed on us now by our "kings" that do not appear, at first glance, to be problematic? That is, what kind of resources would be necessary for Christians today to understand when something is being asked of them that should not be given to those who call themselves our benefactors? This is something of a rhetorical question, for I think we already have the resources—scripture and tradition—necessary to make such careful distinctions. I say scripture *and* tradition for scripture is not self-interpreting. Scripture is often, consciously or not, manipulated to suit our own purposes. I hope to avoid this dilemma, but I can never be too confident that I have accomplished a faithful reading of scripture. I must rely on tradition, as well as a community of faith—an actual body of believers—to help me interpret scripture well. In fact, part of what this book hopes to accomplish is to suggest that some of our best, if not, *the* best resources we have for living as Christians is biographical. The stories of Daniel, Shadrach, Meshach, and Abednego; Ruth, Esther, and Sarah; Hosea, Amos, and Jeremiah;

John, Peter, Mary, and Paul all constitute a tradition of interpretation that is still exemplified in the lives of those who continue to conform their will to God. One of the questions I will explore in this book is whether the witness of law- (and church-) breakers such as Dorothy Day, Clarence Jordan, and the Berrigan brothers maintain a line of continuity with Shadrach, Meshach, and Abendego. Is there a sense in which those who would now stand up against the king are in the same prophetic tradition that produced the aforementioned saints of scripture? If so, what does this mean for how we understand their witness and how, in turn, we live prophetic lives? Specifically, we must ask the question: How are Christians living in a post-Christian climate, though still residing in a nominally Christian culture, capable of discerning when it is time to say, "Be it known to you, O King, that we will not serve your gods . . . ?"

This is a very difficult question to answer. Living under an empire that requires its presidents to swear loyalty to Jesus if they wish to win the presidency dupes us into thinking that loyalty to the empire is synonymous with loyalty to Christ. This conflated sense of dual citizenship is confusing as we too readily assume that what it means to be faithful citizens of the United States of America is harmonious with what it means to be faithful citizens of the church. On the contrary, our allegiance as Christians to the universal church must take precedence over our allegiance to everything else; not only the state, but to anything that would tempt us to domesticate our discipleship (market, family, career, etc.). I wish to challenge such assumptions about citizenship, not because I am anti-empire, but because I am pro-church. This is a matter of missiology, for it is only in our ability to be faithful to the church that we make it possible for the empires of this world to know the resurrected Christ.

That being said my position, for lack of a better word, commits me to what may be called an anarchical posture. Though this may be the case I need to be clear that I do not believe in anything called "anarchy." I do not believe in anarchy/anarchism any more than I believe in democracy or socialism. I am simply unclear as to what it means to profess belief in any political ideology. Given, however, that this is a book that adopts the terminology of anarchism to make certain arguments, it is necessary to examine, in the first chapter, what it means to either adopt, or be adopted by, the language of anarchy. My reasoning is that regardless of whether or not such language can appropriately be referenced in light of Christian discipleship, it is important to at least understand that the pejorative accounts we have imbibed have been, for the most part, neither fair nor faithful to the etymology of the word. I will therefore pave a little space in the first chapter for the discussion of what it might mean to be a Christian anarchist.

It will become clear in the second chapter that I do not advocate so much for an anarchist politics as I do for an apocalyptic politics. Christians live in the secular, the time between times, where God's kingdom is here, yet not in its entirety. We follow a slaughtered yet resurrected Lamb and it is our task to bear witness to this Lamb in a manner that reveals God's in-breaking kingdom. Our manner of life, as it is patterned after the crucified Son of God, appears as nothing more than folly to the world. It cannot be anything other than folly, for it is predicated on a kingdom that is not of this world. It is a kingdom that all other kingdoms must consider a threat, in that it demands a loyalty beyond the temporal. It will be necessary, therefore, to provide a careful examination of this political realm that is appropriately referred to as "upside-down" in relation to the kingdoms of this world. Chapter two will be an exposition of the politics of being a Christian in relation to the privilege of bearing witness to Jesus' present yet coming kingdom.

In order not to privilege theory over practice, the remaining chapters will examine the lives of those Christians who make such reflection, as seen in the first two chapters, possible. The majority of this book is little more than the attempt to re-tell the stories of those who have embodied Christianity well. Chapters three through five will function as brief case studies in the lives of certain twentieth-century figures who have understood and practiced the kingdom of heaven as their primary citizenship. I have narrowed my focus to Christians whose vocation lent them to an anarchical posture *in the sense* that the apparatus of the state was not necessary for their role as followers of Jesus. In order to avoid risking errant claims about Christian anarchists and their relationship to other states, I have chosen to examine only a few Christian anarchists of the twentieth century living directly under the rule of the United States. This is one thing I share with the folks examined in this text, and it is from this sense of having a dual citizenship, one as a member of the body politic known as the United States and the other as a member of the body politic known as the church, that I am required to write.

I will conclude with offering a brief epilogue that takes seriously issues of effectiveness and failure as truthful results of faithfulness. I want to pay special attention to the oft-heard claim that the lives of these radicals were less than effective at making real change. In one of the courses I teach I use Philip Berrigan's autobiography *Fighting The Lamb's War*, and a prominent criticism constantly leveled by the students is that for all of his efforts he accomplished very little. Of course we need to provide a careful examination of what something like "accomplished very little" really means, but I do take seriously their concerns. Moments such as these offer me the opportunity to reflect on how effectiveness, understood as some sort of utilitarian calculus, is not how we gauge faithfulness. Indeed, failure may very well be a sign that one is working with the grain of Jesus' cross. That Jesus had three friends show up to his crucifixion looked like nothing more, at the time, than the grandest failure of all. His cry of "My God, my God why have you forsaken me?" does not exactly scream success either (Matt 27:46). Nevertheless, the resurrection of a slaughtered lamb, slaughtered by the principalities and powers at work within the realm of Roman politics and Jesus' own religious tradition, turns our understanding of success and failure on its head. His resurrection does not render his death, and the path that led to it, moot—it authenticates the path. In doing so, it vindicates what may appear to be the ineffectual and worthless witness of a few radical Christians standing against the world's strongest empire.

Throughout these chapters there will be dialogue with Scripture as well as commentary, both theoretical and biographical, in terms of the relationship between church and state. When appropriate, dialogue with proponents of anarchism will occur, but never as an attempt to replace or reformulate the all-encompassing task of simply *being* a Christian. The task of practicing Christianity in no way hinges upon the Christian embodying anarchism; rather, the fact that baptism alone constitutes the Christian as Christian renders Christian practice anarchical—even in relation to anarchism.

THE TRIPLE AXIS OF EVIL: THE SOUNDTRACK OF OUR LIVES

Human salvation lies in the hands of the creatively maladjusted.

—MARTIN LUTHER KING JR.

The reader will find that I have purposely attempted to focus on those Christian anarchists that have directly addressed Martin Luther King

Jr.'s naming of the triple axis of evil: materialism, racism, and militarism. King astutely understood the interconnections between these three evils. During the height of the Vietnam War, a war King called senseless and liable to the judgment of God, King perceptively put together how such an order required violence and the inequality of classes and races in order to continue. He concluded that a revolution of sorts, the embracing of a modified form of socialism, would have to occur to correct such a culture.[1] The particular genius of the Christians examined in this book is that they recognized the connections between violence, economic greed, and racism. Though each chapter primarily focuses on only one of these three aspects, any study worthy of their lives will reveal how they each resisted King's triple axis of evil. Limited as I am by time and space, I am only going to focus on one particular aspect for chapters three through five. Hopefully, this explains my decision to examine how the Catholic Worker movement calls into question our basic assumptions about money, how a white Baptist farmer from Georgia fights racism, and how a couple of priests nonviolently standing against a violent empire exposes how militant is our predilection for violence.

There are countless other witnesses to the way of Christ throughout the world, and they do not all have to look like these particular individuals. However, I do think that our witness must bear a certain family resemblance. For those examined in this book, there are common threads found throughout their lives that attempt to respond to both injustice and the appropriate giving of one's allegiance. Thus we notice certain commonalities between these chapters in regards to the sharing of goods, the practice of nonviolence, and concerns of racial equality. Most importantly, however, we see a common desire from these individuals to take seriously God's words in the book of Amos:

> I hate, I despise your festivals, and I take no delight in your solemn assemblies . . . Take away from me the noise of your songs; I will not listen to the melody of your harps. But let justice roll down like waters, and righteousness like an ever-flowing stream. (5:21, 23–24)

We live in a culture saturated with mawkish music that passes under the rubric of "Christian" while millions of people attempt to survive without

---

1. For an analysis of the kind of socialism King desired, see Michael Long's *Against Us, But For Us*, 131–69.

adequate housing, food, health care, or clothing. Churches spend time arguing over the best way to "praise" Jesus: Should it be contemporary music full of guitars, drums, and screen-projected clichéd lyrics? Or, should it be the old-time hymns constitutive of organs, hymnals, and one too many "thou's"? I think the debate, while potentially significant, misses the larger point. We praise God not through our singing, but through our ability to care for the widow, the orphan, and the poor. The Christians in this book share the common tendency to see through the festivals, assemblies, and noise of such a banal Christianity as they attempt to participate in the kind of justice and righteousness pleasing to God. It is the kind of justice—for there are many different kinds—that seeks to make visible the city on the hill that cannot be hidden (Matt 5:14). The hope of the Christian is to worship God in such a way that attracts others to God. It is the idea that we might participate in God's incarnation, providing a glimpse of the God that cannot be seen, by the manner in which we love one another (1 John 4:12). In loving one another, even our enemies, we give allegiance to the eternal city. That allegiance is signified in our baptismal practices that constitute the peculiar politics of this city—the politics of "maladjusted creativity." That this city has produced a people through time as various as Catholic clergy arrested for civil disobedience and Southern Baptists excommunicated from their own church, is, I think, a wonderful sign that God's peaceable kingdom respects no denominational boundaries or arbitrarily placed borders, but hinges only upon those who have decided to live into their baptisms.

1 *A Christian Anarchist Politic*

No mistake or crime is more horrible to God than those committed to power.
Why? Because what is official is impersonal, and being impersonal is the greatest
insult that can be paid a person.

—SØREN KIERKEGAARD

The twentieth century was a volatile century. We witnessed countless wars, revolutions, and political ideologies rise and fall in a manner akin to fashion trends on any given high school or college campus. That the twentieth century was the bloodiest century in human history should not be lost on us. We are, supposedly, in an age of freedom, progress, and a retreating barbarism as "civilization" spans the globe. Though the past century was privy to extraordinary changes that resulted in advances in technology, aviation, and medicine, the fact that we are only a button's push away from nuclear destruction renders our advances somewhat moot.

Also indicative of the previous century was the introduction of democracy to large sectors of the world. The early part of the past century was host to many other political theories such as communism, socialism, and anarchism—all of which exercised some very real influence in the United States. Many are probably unaware, for example, that we have the anarchists and socialists to thank for the reduction of ten to sixteen hour work days to eight hour work days. Throughout the century, however, these political ideologies were heavily marginalized. While it is true that there are other cultures still operating under monarchies, theocracies, and communist orders, for the most part it is generally assumed, at least by many of us in the West, that the salvation of the world is dependent upon these countries/cultures adopting, with the aid of the United States, democracy as the only form of politics.

The utilization of salvific language should offend our Christian sensibilities, because in the context being used it is idolatrous. Yet, the fact that the United States is often referred to by her own politicians as *the* "city on the hill" (a moniker supposedly reserved for, and claimed by, Judaism and the church) suggests that there is a soteriological motif attached to the story of this nation-state. To even hint at such language, which is far less than what recent politicians have done, is to attempt to replace the narrative of the church with the narrative of the state. No nation-state is the city on the hill, and any that purport to be are placing themselves outside of the prophetic task of the church that would hold all cities accountable to God's justice. There are no nations capable of rising above the call to repentance, not even the royal nation known as the church. It is not my task in this book to deconstruct such a narrative, but merely to remind Christians that our hope is rooted not in the illusory security offered by the state, and that salvation depends upon the Christian's participation in the reign of the heavenly kingdom.[1] Such participation is not merely an obligation imposed on the Christian for her sake, but for the sake of the world. For if Christians are not Christians, how will the world know of the political reign of God's kingdom?

This immediately begs many questions: What does it mean to be a Christian? Is Christianity merely cognitive assent to specific propositions? That is, is Christianity simply about belief qua belief? "Merely believe and you shall be saved!" shouts many a minister. In contrast, my grandmother was often quick to remind me, perhaps a little too often, that "even Satan believes." She would not allow me to think that the treatment of Christianity as a mental checklist of "yes's and no's" was much of an achievement. I think she was right. Christianity is more than a catalogue of right things to believe, because belief is rendered intelligible not by the things we believe but by the things we do. We live what we profess. We live what we believe. Our convictions are manifested in the way we live. This is not a faith versus works scenario; it is the understanding that unless we obey the teachings of Christ all of our claims to

---

1. For a strong critique of the state's imposed soteriological narrative, see Cavanaugh's *Theopolitical Imagination*.

know him are rendered untruthful (1 John 2:3). Faith, as Jesus makes clear in the Johannine text, is a matter of obedience. Christianity is not so much about what we believe, as it is a path we have chosen to follow. It is an embodied journey with a group of fellow believers/practitioners that strives to provide glimpses of God's peaceable kingdom for the sake of the world. Whether or not we attempt to embody our beliefs is not up for grabs, rather what is at stake is the *manner* in which we go about this communal journey—as this will determine the content and vision of the kingdom that we represent. Our very posture, as a people set apart, will give content to that which we are called to embody. That Christians are to be representatives of God demands not a withdrawal from the world, but a thoroughgoing engagement with it even as we are separate from it. Christians are to engage the same world that was engaged by, and eventually killed, Jesus. It is in the *how* of which we engage such a world that the balance of our precarious witness hangs.

TO BE OR NOT TO BE (OF THE WORLD)

They [disciples] are not of the world, even as I am not of the world.

—JESUS OF NAZARETH

Though we may not be of this world (post-baptism), we are, obviously, in it. There is no retreat, escape, or withdrawal; we are in the world to its very core. Perhaps a preemptive strike at possible critiques is in order: this book does not in any way, shape, or form advocate for some sort of retreat from responsible activity in the public realm. Rather, I wish to pay careful attention to what genuinely constitutes "responsible activity" as well as to not assume too early that we know what the "public realm" signifies. Part of my task will be to suggest that the ecclesial city on journey through the temporal orders of this world must bear witness to the politics of God's kingdom. This means that all of our activity is already inherently political, since Christian witness cannot but bear witness to the kind of God we worship. Concomitantly, it also means that all forms of political governance on this earth—the empires, the monarchies, the nation-states—are parodies of the heavenly kingdom; therefore, what constitutes the public and the political (and our responsibilities to these spaces) are those activities that reflect the substance of

God's kingdom, not earthly ones.[2] Christians are in no way obligated to think or act as if our only political options are those dictated to us by the state. In the United States this means we are freed from the tyranny of having to choose between the so-called left, right, or vastly similar and devastatingly uninteresting, independent. Whether or not one is a Democrat or a Republican is not the issue; what matters is that one is a witness to Christ and the kingdom that is already, though not yet in its fullness, here. This kingdom narrates all other political ideologies as the parasitical creatures they are, since the only kind of goods they can point to are both limited and fundamentally tainted by sin.

The Christian tradition has always claimed that temporal goods, even if they are at best only analogous to the goods of the eternal city, are still good. Neither they, nor the things they seek, are to be confused with the highest good, worship of the Triune God. However, inasmuch as they approximate certain standards of the good—peace and justice, food and shelter—then the temporal city functions as a simulacrum of the heavenly city. Again, this neither replaces the eternal city nor does it demand any allegiance that would conflict with our heavenly allegiance. This simply attests to the realization that the cities of earth can perform approximate services in relation to the good. It is for this reason that when the Israelites found themselves in exile the prophet Jeremiah instructed them to build houses, plant gardens, and marry—all within the confines of their diasporic existence. In doing so, the exiled Jews "seek the welfare of the city" that is not even their own (29:7). This "nation-less" people contribute to both the good of the temporal city for the sake of believer and non-believer alike. What is important here is that this is not a mere observation of how to best "get by." The seeking of the peace of the city as exiles is a purposeful command from God that tells us something about who God is. The seeking of the welfare of the city as the chosen yet exiled people of God is vocational—it is a matter of missiology. The very posture itself—an exilic body of people making their homes in a foreign land—is a socially embodied witness. Exile is the means by which God's people evangelize the world.[3]

---

2. For a possible critique of such thinking, one might look toward Oliver O'Donovan's *Desire of the Nations*, which suggests that there are legitimate forms of earthly governance despite a fallen creation.

3. For a detailed account of what it means for exile to be a missionary posture, see John Howard Yoder's *For the Nations*.

In a very practical sense we must ask how is it that Christians are to seek the peace of the city while maintaining their identity as God's people without falling prey to the temptation to *secure* the peace of the city. Though I will address this specific concern in the following chapter, much of what I am attempting to do, through the lives remembered in this book, is to show how to seek the peace of the city without seeking to gain a hold on such peace. This means that we must be willing to let go, to live lives out of control. Being in control is a hard habit to break as so many of us want to force on the world what we understand to be the truth. Such desires, however, pervert the kind of peace we are called to seek. I intend to show that Christian allegiance to the heavenly city presumes an exilic posture that confers a missionary stance, a nomadic and diasporic posture, ultimately even an *anarchic* posture that best gives some semblance of what it is that we are seeking.[4]

"BY THIS I MEAN ANYTHING BUT DISORDER"

The worst thing in this world, next to anarchy, is government.

—HENRY WARD BEECHER

It is important to clarify what I mean when I say that being a Christian may demand an anarchic posture. The word "anarchy" generally brings to mind a world without order, one of chaos and destruction. In his foreword to Herbert Read's *Anarchy and Order*, Howard Zinn reflects on this sentiment and quickly turns it on its head:

> The word *anarchy* unsettles most people in the Western world; it suggests disorder, violence, uncertainty. We have good reason for fearing those conditions, because we have been living with them for a long time, not in anarchist societies (there have never been any) but in exactly those societies most fearful of anarchy—the powerful nation-states of modern times.[5]

We may take Zinn to task for suggesting there have never been any anarchist societies in history (there have been many), but he is correct to sug-

---

4. A similar argument is made in my book *The Purple Crown*, where I claim that martyrs embody the ultimate exilic posture inasmuch as they are not only exiled from the city walls, but are exiled from life.

5. Read, *Anarchy and Order*, ix.

gest that it is by no means clear that in a world without governments we would be any less violent and oppressive than we currently are. Though the presence of governments justifies its place by our perpetuated fears that without them we would descend into chaos and violence, it cannot be ruled out *a priori* that an anarchist society, a society predicated upon voluntary associations, would be any more chaotic, violent, or uncertain than our present situation.

Semantically, the word "anarchy" means something to the effect of the state of being without a government or a ruler. Anarchy is derived from the Greek, *an* indicating without, plus *arche* implying government or authority. The first to take upon himself the moniker "anarchist" was the nineteenth-century French philosopher Pierre-Joseph Proudhon. In his treatise *What is Property?*, Proudhon adopts the term anarchist after describing, ironically, how the church disregards the teachings of Jesus so that they can justify the ownership of private property:

> What is to be the form of government in the future? I hear some of my younger readers reply: "Why, how can you ask such a question? You are a republican."
>
> "A republican! Yes; but that word specifies nothing. *Res publica*; that is, the public thing. Now, whoever is interested in public affairs—no matter what form of government—may call himself a republican. Even kings are republicans."
>
> "Well! You are a democrat?"
>
> "No."
>
> "What! You would have a monarchy?"
>
> "No."
>
> "A Constitutionalist?"
>
> "God forbid."
>
> "You are then an aristocrat?"
>
> "Not at all!"
>
> "You want a mixed form of government?"
>
> "Still less."
>
> "What are you, then?"
>
> "I am an anarchist."

"Oh! I understand you; you speak satirically. This is a hit at the government."

"By no means. I have just given you my serious and well-considered profession of faith. Although a firm friend of order, I am (in the full force of the term) an anarchist. Listen to me."[6]

In the above dialogue Proudhon suggests that part of his "profession of faith" entails friendship with order. In order to stress this reality he occasionally spelled the word anarchy as "an-archy" in order to suggest the possibility of human existence without the presence of an official governing body. It is what the Italian anarchist Errico Malatesta referred to as "the state of a people without any constituted authority."[7] Anarchy, therefore, assumes no inherent connotations of being anti- or against anything. Rather, the "an" prior to the "archy" plainly suggests a lack of something. In this case, it suggests a lack of governmental authority. It is indeed a rather large conceptual leap to assume that the absence of a governing body necessarily entails disorder. For many anarchists, it is the exact opposite; it is the enforced rule of the few over the majority that produces the conditions that cause disorder. Chaos is not what the anarchist desires. When Proudhon spoke of the term anarchy (which he eventually dropped because of both the unfair and unnecessary pejorative connotations that its opponents attached to it), he said he meant "anything but disorder."[8] Rather, for Proudhon, and the early classical anarchists, anarchy is not the protest against order, it is the protest against the kind of (dis)order created and perpetuated by the nation-state. If anarchists are against anything, they are against the kind of chaos that arises from what they see as the unnatural relationships that occur through governments and its people. For anarchists such as Proudhon and Malatesta, to name just a few, disorder arises whenever power becomes centralized in the hands of the few, creating the conditions by which humans become little more than objects to be controlled/governed—even if it is for their "own benefit."[9]

---

6. Proudhon, *What is Property?* 270.

7. Horowitz, *The Anarchists*, 71.

8. Guerin, *Anarchism*, 42.

9. Notice the parallel with Jesus' words in Mark 10:42–44 where he demands that we are to be nothing like those Gentiles who claim to be benefactors and lord their power over others.

For the secular anarchist, anarchy is not just the absence of government. Rather, the term is employed to provide an alternative vision of the good. The anarchist assumes that governments are the actual sources of the vast majority of our social ills. Anarchism is that "doctrine which contends that government is the source of most of our social troubles and that there are viable alternative forms of voluntary organization. And by further definition the *anarchist* is the man who sets out to create a society without government."[10] The latter part of this quote is particularly instructive as the anarchist realizes the importance of what it means to participate responsibly within the realm of society. The common notion that anarchists reject society is incorrect insofar as it is the anarchist who understands the significance of society becoming a living, thriving entity amidst the lack of a governing body. This is what Malatesta is referring to when he considered anarchism to be synonymous with "natural order, . . . complete liberty with complete solidarity."[11] Anarchists are not against something called society, they are for the kind of society in which humanity can flourish. To this end, the anarchist thinks that it is through the process of freely chosen voluntary associations that humans can better gather, live, and exist in a way not possible through coercive governing. This is what they mean when they suggest anarchism represents a natural order. A natural order, in this case, refers to an order by which the domination of the many by the few is abolished.

In the eleventh edition of the Encyclopedia Brittanica, the well-known anarcho-communist Peter Kropotkin was asked to contribute by writing an article on anarchism. He wrote, "Anarchism . . . is the name given to a principle or theory of life and conduct under which society is conceived without government."[12] Anarchism, Kropotkin is suggesting, is the idea that people can better manage their lives—albeit collectively—without the interference of government. This is intended to be a constructive, not destructive theory toward human life. Rather, it is when humans rule over others that destruction occurs. Kropotkin imagines the possibility of a body of people living in such a way that no order from "above" would be necessary. This does not stem from a purely romanticized account of human nature as much as it originates from the idea that humans can

---

10. Woodcock, *The Anarchist Reader*, 11.

11. Horowitz, *The Anarchists*, 73.

12. Krimerman and Perry, *Patterns of Anarchy*, 3.

cooperatively manage themselves. In this regard it can be deduced that anarchist theory presupposes that a highly organized structure would need to take the place of centralized forms of coercive power. The twentieth-century Russian anarchist Volin agrees:

> A mistaken—or more often, deliberately inaccurate—interpretation alleges that the libertarian concept means the absence of all organization. This is entirely false: it is not a matter of 'organization' or 'non-organization', but of two different principles of organization . . . Of course, say the anarchists, society must be organized. However, the new organization . . . must be established freely, socially, and, above all, from below.[13]

Likewise, almost all anarchists have construed their thoughts in such a way as to convince others that they are productive and not antagonistic toward society. Their particular antagonism is directed towards the *kind* of society sustained under the maintenance of the nation-state. It is this latter construction, argues the anarchist, which treats humans as mere means for the endless machinations of those in charge. Create a society free from the domination of the few over the many (or the many over the few), and the conditions that make for chaos and violence will, hopefully, dissipate. Though the Christian rightly criticizes the anarchist for adopting a posture of almost unbridled optimism in regards to the goodness of human nature (given the account of sin within Christian theology), the anarchist can rightly criticize the Christian for not living into the resurrection made possible by the kingdom that is already, yet not fully, here. To this point, we shall return. It is enough, for the moment, to agree with the anarchist who reminds us how demonic power over others routinely manifests itself. After thousands of years of recorded history in which the vast majority of humans have suffered much by the very few who have gained because of their sufferings, anarchists simply want to tip the scales in a manner that favors all humans.

Despite the anarchists' claims to the contrary, anarchism has generally been construed by its opponents as a pathway descending into chaos, confusion, and violence. Though it is the case that some anarchists have both advocated and practiced acts of violence, the term itself does not, semantically, demand anything of the sort. If violence or chaos does occur it is not because anarchism is synonymous with these terms, but because

---

13. Guerin, *Anarchism*, 43.

those who wish to achieve or enact an anarchistic world have employed violence as a means to affect an anarchistic condition. The state of anarchy cannot necessarily be identified with the means by which some have attempted to attain it unless we also wish to re-configure what we mean by terms like freedom and democracy (then again, perhaps we should). More importantly, it is a mistake to assume that all anarchists willfully employ, or are open to the use of, violence to achieve a desired end. Such tactics, though they are *unconditionally* the norm for the archist, are by no means a given for the anarchist. For the archist to criticize the anarchist for the possible resort to violence is hypocritical, as all archists must assume the place of violence in any governing body. This is not an assumption indicative of anarchism. Some anarchists even argue that the employment of violence is at odds with the world they wish to convey and demand a thoroughgoing pacifism.[14] There is much debate around the issue of violence, and there is no consensus in terms of whether or not anarchism as a political theory must either assume or reject pacifism. I merely point this out in order to suggest that the specter of the violent anarchist, while there have been some in history, pales in comparison to the historical reality of the violent archist. Indeed, one wonders whether or not those who assume the necessity of government can even entertain a position of nonviolence.

I make these comments not because this is a book on anarchism (this is a book on Christian discipleship), but because there has been a long-standing bias against such language. I only want to suggest that such deprecatory associations are unfounded, and that if one employs the language of anarchy to describe Christian politics one is neither treading on anti-political nor anti-Christian grounds. Though I will occasionally lean on certain anarchists' insights, I want primarily to be able to employ this language without drudging up false connotations. At the same time, I hope to be very clear as to my own bias about how this term can and should be employed to describe Christian activity. I imagine this will not sit well with many contemporary secular anarchists. Anarchism has generally implied not only a lack of belief in God but also an outright rejection of any god or religion, as religion, many

14. See, for instance, Ira Chernus's chapter on pacifist anarchists in her *American Nonviolence*, 56–74; John Howard Yoder's section on anarchistic pacifism in his book *Nevertheless*, 116–17, 128–29; Jacques Ellul's *Anarchy and Christianity*; and Vernard Eller's *Christian Anarchy*.

anarchists suggest, hinders our freedom in a manner akin to govern-ments.[15] Ammon Hennacy tells of the meeting he and Dorothy Day, co-founder of the Catholic Worker Movement, had with a number of Italian atheist anarchists on this very point. Hennacy describes their meeting as it took place in 1941 in the home of one of these anarchists.[16] He says that though they all remained in good spirits throughout their rather exasperating conversations, their hosts consistently demanded that the two Christians drop the language of anarchism. For the Italian anarchists, anarchism represented the rejection of all authority. Day and Hennacy countered that it was their submission to the authority of Christ that made it possible for them to be anarchical in relation to the powers of the world. The atheists complimented them on their ability to sacrifice so much in regards to their resistance to the state, but thought they were both foolish and naïve for being subservient to the author-ity of the church. Hennacy responded that he was only as faithful to church authorities as these anarchists were to those they so desperately revere—Berkman, Bakunin and Goldman. Hennacy's point is an im-portant one. Flight from some sort of authority is not possible. These, and all anarchists, are in a tradition in which there are certain thinkers who carry far more weight, far more authority, than others. There are no non-traditioned responses. We all speak from somewhere because we are not ahistorical beings. It will be my contention that precisely be-cause of one's active belief in the triune God Christians are freed from the principalities and powers of the world in a way that might escape other anarchists. This is, perhaps, most visible in the indebtedness that many anarchists have in relation to modern philosophy.

For example, within these principalities and powers is the political theory liberalism. In the seventeenth century various political theorists,

15. Cf. Guerin's two volume edited set, *No Gods, No Masters*, as well as Mikhail Bakunin's *God and The State*. Despite the incongruity that most anarchists find with the notion of obedience to God (as this goes against the primarily individualistic/liberal notion that self-rule is the only natural course of rule), Proudhon argued that in an an-archist world freedom of religion must be guaranteed. After all, what kind of anarchist tells another what they can and cannot believe? On another level, others have argued that the anti-authoritarian attitudes of certain religious bodies prior to the development of anarchism is not synonymous with this term. That is undoubtedly the case, however part of what my argument hinges on is that the Christians listed in this book are not anti-authoritarian, rather they are pro-ecclesia.

16. This is story is located in Krimerman and Perry's *Patterns of Anarchy*, 48–52.

most notably the British empiricist John Locke, promoted individual liberty to the level of primacy in matters of government. Liberalism, as a political ideology/theory, suggests that in our natural state we are, or at least should be, free to order our actions any way we choose and that any prohibition against such freedom requires justification. Governing bodies, if they are to be just, must adhere to such an account of our natural state, and its policies should reflect such an adherence. Humans, via representative or participatory forms of democracy, engage primarily in those activities or alliances that behoove one another. The governed engage in social contracts with both one another and their respective governments. For the good of all, certain activities of the individual must be limited. This is necessary for matters of social order that has as its highest goal the pursuit of liberty for each individual. From this tradition evolved language such as autonomy, free choice, individualism, and the inner self. Such language is quite apparent in our liberal democracy where both the right and the left assume, as matters of common sense, the objective truth and corresponding realties of such language. They primarily differ on to what extent certain human actions should be justifiably controlled; otherwise both the right and the left are liberals in the classic sense of the word.

Anarchism is basically an expansion on some of the fundamental precepts of modern political theory.[17] Many anarchists will agree with the basic insights of liberal theorists such as Locke, Hume or Rousseau. Anarchists often employ the language of rights, choice, and autonomy with absolute uncritical acceptance. The primary objection that anarchism has toward political liberalism is the assumption that behavior needs to be controlled by a governing body of people (whether elected or not). Many liberal theorists share the common judgment that humans are both by nature free and good. Anarchists tend to extend such an account by suggesting that it is the exertion of control on these free and good entities that is the cause of much human misery. Although the anarchist wishes to be free from the kind of governing bodies created in moder-

17. Some anarchists would disagree with this statement. In his book *The Political Animal*, Stephen R. L. Clark argues that anarchism has its roots in the political philosophy of Aristotle. There have also been numerous communities who lived in a manner that could be described as anarchical well prior to the modern age. Nevertheless, to use the language of anarchism in these cases, while avoiding the grammar of speech that led to its rise, is to speak anachronistically and to be found 'guilty' of one of the cardinal virtues of modernity: ahistoricism.

nity (nation-states), they are not free from the philosophical conditions that paved the way for the nation-state.[18] It is in this sense that Christian anarchists are capable of providing their secular kin a witness that is not being determined by the very thing that gave rise to anarchism. The Christian anarchist is neither determined nor created by the forces of liberalism, but via the crucifixion and resurrection of Jesus. Given this reality, Christians are liberated from any and all political theories, including anarchism, which are contingent upon fallen historical forces for their intelligibility. Due to Jesus' resurrection, and the believer's hope of sharing in his resurrection, Christians are freed from the constraints of time itself while being freed into Christ's apocalyptic mode of timefulness, thus being liberated to enact or perform an ontology of *peace*. We are free to be in the world like no other because Jesus' resurrection has redeemed all of creation. We have the time and space to be free in a manner unimaginable by others as our freedom extends beyond the secular (the time between times). This is not a call away from participation in temporal orders, rather it changes the discourse altogether. Christians can act in this time and space unlike any other people because they are already freed from the tyranny of death. What can the world possibly do to a people who are already resurrected? To live into this resurrection is to live free—including free from the restraints of an historically contingent political theory like anarchism.

JESUS, NOT PROUDHON (OR GOLDMAN, KROPOTKIN, ETC.)

Christ was a free man, the freest of the sons of men.

—NICHOLAS BERDYAEV

Despite being an ideology that espouses the absence of government as a better means to adjudicate the "natural" forces of freedom with humanity, anarchism is but another political ideology. It is what William Stringfellow referred to as a lapsed manifesto of what some have turned to in the absence of a viable alternative.[19] I will, however, continue to use

18. I am indebted to Halden Doerge for reminding me that these philosophical conditions did not *simply* pave the way for the nation-state, rather they are the very foundation of its conceptual architecture. The notion that such edifices could be used to create or imagine a different vision of human life is simply not possible, or even intelligible.

19. Stringfellow, *Conscience and Obedience*, 55–74. Unfortunately, Stringfellow

this term because Christians are free to live anarchically even in relation to anarchism.[20] The Christians of the early church (up to the fourth century), the various ascetics and monks throughout the middle ages, the Waldensians of the twelfth and thirteenth centuries, Peter Chelčický and the Bohemian Brethren in the fifteenth century, the development of the Anabaptists in the sixteenth century, the English Diggers or True Levellers of the seventeenth century, Tolstoy and Ballou in the nineteenth century, or the Catholic Workers of the twentieth century: these are but a few examples of a history of people whose only authority was the path laid out for them in the manner of a cross. These Christians do not necessarily need the resources of the secular anarchists (though, their employment of such should be, and often is, welcomed), nor do they require an object of protest in which to base their convictions. The convictions of the Christian stem from the nexus of practices or forms of life derivative of such practices that include the Eucharist, baptism and the proclaimed Word. It is at the Eucharistic table where all of us remember the broken body and spilled blood of Christ that makes our redemption, and participation in the divine life, possible. It is because of the atonement that we are who we are as well as whom we need to be for the world. If that leads to a posture that some may call anarchical, then so be it. Our identity, however, and thankfully, is by no means dependent upon such an appellation.

In his essay *Slavery and Freedom*, Nicholas Berdyaev discusses the conditions necessary for both physical and existential escape from tyranny and bondage. Though much of his work, like many of the leading Christian anarchist theorists (e.g., Ballou, and Tolstoy), is not always aligned with Christian orthodoxy, Berdyaev's theology reminds us that there is only one guarantor of freedom: "God is the guarantee of the freedom of personality from the enslaving power of nature and society, of the Kingdom of Caesar and of the object world."[21] As beings freed from the Kingdom of Caesar we are capable of enacting the cruciform and resurrected politic of Jesus—that freest of all free humans. Caesar's politic is

---

chooses to make a distinction between anarchism and anarchy that I think is unfounded. He views the former as a distinctive kind of political ideology while the latter he uses in the generic sense of referring to chaos. I am unclear as to what necessitates this move.

20. Laurence Veysey notes in his book *The Communal Experience* that it was originally religious impulses that created the possibilities for anarchy (vii).

21. This is quoted in Krimerman and Perry's *Patterns of Anarchy*, 153.

a politic of slavery. This is not because we are ruled, but because to be a ruler is to be enslaved to this world. Berdyaev comments on this reality:

> Caesar, the hero of imperialism, is a slave; he is the slave of the world, the slave of the will to power, the slave of the human masses, without whom he cannot realize his will to power. The master knows only the height to which his slaves raise him. Caesar knows only the height to which the masses raise him. But the slaves, and the masses, also overthrow all masters and Caesars. Freedom is freedom not only from the masses but from the slaves also.[22]

The freedom that Christian anarchism prizes, at least within this book, is not to simply be confused with liberation or emancipation from tyrannous regimes and orders. Though it is this, it is much more as it seeks to free those rulers who are themselves enslaved to this will to power. The Christian anarchist is not one who just does not want to be told what to do, as the juvenile anarchist would have it, but is the one willing to embody the kind of freedom that poses an alternative to those in charge so that they too can know genuine freedom. Sometimes, as we will see through the witness of Dorothy Day and Clarence Jordan, such freedom takes the posture of servitude toward others. This may seem paradoxical as the anarchist is supposed to be one modeling freedom—freedom from *both* ruling *and* being ruled. Alan Lewis captures this handily in his description of the political threat posed by Jesus:

> What damage could be done to the mighty structures of the empire by one who gave Caesar his due, who scorned the bigotry which hated an infidel and punished the ungodly, and who pictured a kingdom of freedom, peace, and love in which the distinction between friend and foe would lose all meaning? Yet, with their unseeing eyes, the Romans had rightly perceived a radical and dangerous subversion—with clearer intuition, it seems, than those who still characterize the preaching of Jesus as spiritual and therefore not political. What, in fact, could be more 'political,' a more complete and basal challenge to the kingdoms of this world, to its generals and its lords, both to those who hold power and to those who would seize it, than one who says that his kingdom is not of this world, and yet prays that the kingdom of his Father will come and his will be done on earth. This is an aspiration for the world more revolutionary, a disturbance of the status quo more

22. Ibid., 157.

seismic, an allegiance more disloyal, a menace more intimidating, than any program which simply meets force with force and matches loveless injustice with loveless vengeance. Here is a whole new ordering of human life, as intolerable to insurrectionists as to oppressors. It promises that forgiveness, freedom, love, and self-negation, in all their feeble ineffectiveness, will prove more powerful and creative than every system and every countersystem which subdivides the human race into rich and poor, comrades and enemies, insiders and outsiders, allies and adversaries. What could an earthly power, so in love with power as to divinize it in the person of its emperor, do with such dangerous powerlessness but capture and destroy it? It could change everything were it not extinguished, and speedily."[23]

Yet, this is the great scandal, or as some may have it the folly, of Christian anarchism: it is the freedom to be as that freest of all humans. Berdyaev claims that Jesus was "free from the world; He was bound only by love."[24] It this kind of freedom that we are privileged to enact. This demands more than an anarchistic politic, this requires an apocalyptic politic. Apocalypticism, as a Christian politic, is the subject of the next chapter.

23. Lewis, *Between Cross and Resurrection*, 49–50.
24. Krimerman and Perry, *Patterns of Anarchy*, 157.

2 *Apocalyptic Politics*

[M]y relation to him [the emperor] is one of freedom;
for I have but one true Lord . . .

—Tertullian

The reunification of creation, argues St. Augustine, depends on Christians living as faithful citizens. In his masterpiece *The City of God*, Augustine demands that Christians live in this world as good stewards of creation, as participants in the good of the common life, and as worshippers of the triune God.[1] Such participation, such worship, is necessary not simply for the sake of the Christian, but for the sake of the non-Christian. For if the Christian neglects God doxologically (can they still be called a Christian?) then the world loses its resources for even knowing it is the world—much less becoming an active participant in the goodness of God. The church, as John Howard Yoder notes, "precedes the world epistemologically."[2] Yoder is suggesting that the category of world does not even function without the church's narration of such a category.[3] This means that if we fail to partake in the economy of the triune God, then we fail to offer the world the ability for it to be able to understand itself as world—denying it the opportunity to participate in a redeemed order. Therefore, we cannot abandon nor withdraw from the fallen goodness of creation, but must enact that which we are called for its very redemption. This means that our very participation in the world is missiological. Christians, laity or clerical, are commissioned to make disciples of all nations (Matt 28:19), and we do this by bearing witness to the one who

1. Augustine, *The City of God*, 872–82.
2. Yoder, *The Priestly Kingdom*, 11.
3. This is putting it in a way that is more akin to Hauerwas' reading of Yoder than Yoder himself, yet I think it is not totally unfaithful. The resources that Yoder is most indebted to (the Radical Reformation) tend to assume the kind of church/world dichotomy that makes possible a comment such as "the church precedes the world epistemologically."

sent us. There simply is no escape from the temporal order as we must not abandon it, but provide it with an alternative. The enactment and performance of Christianity, and her attendant account of citizenship, is absolutely crucial for the proper presentation of the church's witness.

However, what constitutes Christian citizenship? Does Christian citizenship differ from the citizenship of a non-Christian? Do Christians operate with a monistic or a dualistic account of citizenship? The late second century *Epistle to Diognetus* is instructive:

> Christians are distinguished from the rest of men neither by country nor by language nor by customs. For nowhere do they dwell in cities of their own; they do not use any strange form of speech or practice a singular mode of life. . . . But while they dwell in both Greek and barbarian cities, each as his lot was cast, and follow the customs of the land in dress and food and other matters of living, they show forth the remarkable and admittedly strange order of their own citizenship. They live in fatherlands of their own, but as aliens. They share all things as citizens, and suffer all things as strangers. Every foreign land is their fatherland, and every fatherland a foreign land. . . . They pass their days on earth, but they have their citizenship in heaven.[4]

Implicit in this passage is the argument that Christians maintain something of a dual identity. This should not be understood in the sense of the modern fixation with the self and those existential realities that lay claim to it. This text is referring to the reality that there are multiple narratives at work in our lives, many of which attempt to lay a primary claim on us. Yet, there is an identity, which comes with baptism, an identity of giftedness that narrates all other narratives. In the case of politics, who we are is not simply bound to our national identities, but our status as Christians, and the citizenship this entails, renders our citizenship on earth as something altogether different from the non-Christian.[5] According to the

---

4. *The Epistle to Diognetus*, 79–80. Book V. 1–9. The writer of this letter continues by drawing an analogy between the body and the soul and the Christian and the world. Just as the soul is in the body but not of the body so are Christians in the world but not of the world. Though this is not the place to argue either for or against the author's antagonistic dichotomy between the soul and the body, the analogy is useful insofar as it presents a vivid image of what it means to be in the world but not of the world.

5. This is not to suggest that Christianity is the only "religion" ("culture" may be a better word) that may be antithetical to earthly forms of citizenship. Cultural narratives such as Buddhism, Islam, and Judaism, among many other smaller faith traditions (e.g.,

anonymous writer of the above letter, Christians share all things as citizens yet suffer as strangers; every land the Christian inhabits is treated as if it is her homeland though it remains foreign to her; the Christian lives on earth, yet her true residency is in heaven. This is to say that Christians live in the here and now, yet recognize the ephemeral status of earthly cities. We operate with the distinctive posture as a political society within a host of other political societies.

This is not, at least within the early church, an unusual account of the peculiarity of Christian citizenship. Justin Martyr attempts to clarify in his *First Apology* that Christians, when speaking of a rival kingdom, are not talking about a "human one," but of the kingdom of God—of which all Christians are citizens.[6] Origen is of a similar mind when he argues that the best citizens of the empire are those who first and foremost are citizens of heaven as they "do more good to their countries than the rest of mankind, since they educate the citizens and teach them to be devoted to God, the guardian of their city; and they take those who have lived good lives in the most insignificant cities up to a divine and heavenly city."[7] For Origen, the path to the divine and heavenly city is through the church (which, for him, is synonymous with the telling phrase "God's country"). Tertullian claims that the reason Christians are considered public enemies is because they refuse to indulge the empire in its idolatrous efforts to procure the total allegiance of its citizens over against the God who created all.[8] The one worthy of worship is neither the emperor who rules the empire nor the empire that wishes to rule the bodies of its citizens; rather, the only one worthy of worship is the one who rules the emperor: the God of Christianity. Tertullian's apology is stemming from his attempt to display the "peculiarities of the Christian society" in which one such peculiarity is the fact that the only commonwealth the Christian knows is not the tribal sectarian nature of states and empires, but the

---

Jehovah's Witnesses, the Masons, etc.) can and often do call into question such conflicting loyalties.

6. Justin Martyr, *The First Apology*, XI. It is interesting to note that in the apologies of Justin Martyr, as well as Tertullian, these thinkers genuinely thought that their status as Christians, as citizens in another kingdom, was the best possible news for the Roman Empire. Justin goes on to state: "And more than all other men are we your helpers and allies in promoting peace . . . ." XII.

7. Origen, *Against Celsus*, 74–75, in O'Donovan and Lockwood O' Donovan's *From Irenaeus to Grotius*, 45.

8. Tertullian, *Apology*, XXXIII–XXXVI.

whole universe.[9] For as a people of the "universe" Christians give no loyalty to anything other than God, and, therefore, Christians respect and honor all of creation—not just one small geographical sector. It is clear that Tertullian is not against the empire or is even anti-Roman; rather, he is simply defined by that which he is for—which is total obedience to God.

For these early Christians, as well as the majority of the theologians, bishops, and martyrs that constituted the first three hundred years of Christianity, almost all were of one mind in their insistence that all governments derive their power from God.[10] This means that the Christian's primary allegiance is not to any one empire, but to the God of all empires. It is such thinking that renders intelligible Tertullian's claim to pagan Roman citizens that "Caesar is more ours than yours."[11] Such loyalty and allegiance places the Christian, as the *Epistle to Diognetus* notes, in a peculiar position in terms of the various cities of the world.

Such thinking clearly did not arrive in a theological vacuum. Much of the intuitive theologizing of the early church took as its starting place the writings of both St. Peter and St. Paul. In the writings of Peter we find reference made to the nature of Christians being both "aliens" and "exiles" in this world (1 Pet 2:11). This language follows a previous passage in which Peter refers to Christians as a "chosen race, a royal priesthood, a holy nation, God's own people . . . " (1 Pet 2:9). For Peter, Christians are a nation unto themselves. Though they are a nation of exiles and aliens they are still a nation.

Paul, too, exemplifies this thought as he writes to the Philippian church that their citizenship is not in Rome but "is in heaven" (Phil 3:20).

9. Ibid., XXXVIII.

10. The first church historian Eusebius recounts the martyrdom narrative of Sanctus "who with magnificent, superhuman courage nobly withstood the entire range of human cruelty." Eusebius claims that regardless of the torture Sanctus was forced to endure, he refused to offer his name, race or birthplace. For Sanctus, these things were of absolutely no significance. To every question Sanctus was asked, he consistently replied with one answer: 'I am a Christian.' "This he proclaimed," notes Eusebius, "over and over again, instead of name, birthplace, nationality, and everything else, and not another word did the heathen hear from him." Eusebius, *The History of the Church from Christ to Constantine*, 141–42. Though issues of nationality and citizenship were of importance to those Christians seeking to, literally, 'keep their heads', for the martyrs discussion of temporal citizenship provided the opportunity to merely name one's overriding citizenship which was to Christ and his kingdom.

11. Tertullian, *Apology*, XXXIII.

Though Rome, like any other power, is a power derivative from God (Col 1:15–17), the people of God, not the emperor, president, or monarch, are the primary bearers of God's word (Eph 2–3). Paul claims that though we were once aliens to the commonwealth known as Israel (Eph 2:12), we have now been engrafted into their story in order that, through the church, we may make known the "wisdom of God in its rich variety . . . to the rulers and authorities in the heavenly places" (Eph. 3:10–11). Paul is saying that not only does the continuation of the story of Israel through the church bear God's message to the world, but even the powers within heaven are privy to the story we tell. It is hard to imagine being any more public or political than that.

As a holy nation instilled with the mission to tell/show the world God's redemptive story for all of creation, Christians face the problem of adulterating their heavenly citizenship with their earthly citizenship. That many of us claim, or are required to claim, citizenship within a particular nation-state while simultaneously claiming citizenship in heaven gives us a sense of dual citizenship. However, it is *how* we enact this dual citizenship that determines who the primary storyteller is (church or state), and in such an adjudication of different body politics we bear witness to that of which we ultimately find to be of greatest significance. Do our loyalties lie with the church that exists throughout all other political bodies, or do our loyalties lie with any number of nation-states, which must be understood as sectarian in comparison with the universal church? The kind of witness displayed will be contingent upon the locating of one's primary narrative. If it is the case that it is the church that narrates all other loyalties, we should not assume that this would necessitate derisive or apathetic practices toward the earthly city; instead, the citizen of heaven will practice subordination to the earthly cities as commanded by both Paul and Peter (Romans 13 & 1 Pet 2:15). At the same time, subservience is by no means synonymous with obedience. Peter demands that we "must obey God rather than any human authority" and that any time we are asked to participate in an action that is contrary to the will of God we have no other choice but to show the error of those in charge by obeying God (Acts 5:29). Such a journey may not always be a pleasant one—for we have the paradigmatic example, as found in Jesus, of what happens when one speaks the truth—yet, if we are to do as Christ commands, to take up his cross and follow him, then we must not avoid the performance of the politic known as the church.

If the church is to be successful at enacting this cruciform politic, then it must begin to take its own self, its own practices and habits, seriously. It must also come to terms with how it operates as politically different from the world. For example, if as Christians we think that what it means to be political is to either vote Republican or Democrat (or independent for that matter) then we have already both conceded and privileged the world's politics as *the* politic. The church, however, is constituted by an entirely different manner of looking at politics because our starting point, the crucified Jesus, *is* a politic. He is the King of kings, Lord of lords, the Prince of peace who manifests the in-breaking Kingdom of God. This is not mere figurative language but defines the very nature of what it means to be the kind of creature whose primary allegiance is to this Kingdom. Our politics are the politics of this Kingdom, and this means that the church must be a confessing church that is not so much caught up in being "politically responsible" as defined by the policy makers of Capitol Hill, but by the way of the Lamb that was slaughtered by similar policy makers two thousand years ago. Our politics stem from the cross that the politics of this world erected.

This places the Christian, as the servant who is not better than her master, in a peculiar position. If the church is to be the church of the cross then what we may find out is that, just as the life and death of Jesus revealed, "the world, for all its beauty, is hostile to the truth."[12] For our witness, our very posture is a mode of being that cannot but lead to hostility from the world. If our politic is truly in the shape of a cross then we should not expect to be well received as this is the very form our witness must take. Theologians Stanley Hauerwas and William Willimon claim that the cross

> . . . is not a sign of the church's quiet, suffering submission to the powers-that-be, but rather the church's revolutionary participation in the victory of Christ over those powers. The cross is not a symbol for general human suffering and oppression. Rather, *the cross is a sign of what happens when one takes God's account of reality more seriously than Caesar's.* The cross stands as God's and our eternal no to the powers of death, as well as God's eternal yes to humanity, God's remarkable determination not to leave us to

---

12. Hauerwas and Willimon, *Resident Aliens*, 47.

our devices. The overriding political task of the church is to be the community of the cross.[13]

The people of the cross are at odds with those that erect such crosses. Both operate under two different politics. Neither is a mode of withdrawal from the world, rather both exemplify two contrasting ways of being in the world. The cross-bearers are every bit as public and political as those that condemn them to a cross.

APOCALYPTIC, NOT APOLITICAL

The whole point of an apocalyptic style is precisely an unwillingness to grant history a status apart from God: It is God's-story.

—DAVID O'TOOLE

The politic of the church, however, is not just a crucified politic, it is a risen politic. Christians are to follow the slaughtered Lamb for this is the One from which our politic is derivative. This slaughtered Lamb is a victorious Lamb. Through the death of Jesus and his subsequent resurrection the powers that are fallen in this world, and which continue to rebel and wage war against him and his followers are already defeated. In his revelation, St. John claims that the world will continue to engage war with the Lamb despite the fact that these powers have already been conquered (Rev 12:11). As witnesses to this slaughtered yet victorious Lamb, Christians reflect the defeat of the powers of this earth by being true to that which we know to be true: Christ's victory. It is for this reason that John claims that Jesus' followers will also share in his victory: "[T]hey will make war on the Lamb, and the Lamb will conquer them, for He is Lord of lords and King of kings, and those with him are called and chosen and faithful." (Rev 17:14) Those who follow the slaughtered Lamb may or may not find themselves slain, but they will most certainly find themselves to be victorious. This is because Christians do not simply bow to any king, but to the King who is king of all kings.

The way of Christ demands absolute obedience to only this one Lord. This makes our every act of worship a moment in politics. There is no separation between our worship and the response this engenders from the powers that are in rebellion against Christ. We are told to "come

13. Ibid. (Italics mine.)

out" of Babylon (Rev 18:4) in order to avoid participating in her sins. This does not mean that we must physically exile ourselves from the city (for that would just put us in a different Babylon), but that the call of the church is to discern the character and content of where we are and what this means for how we are to distance ourselves from imperial seduction.[14] It is simply not possible to be a citizen of multiple cities without a compromise of one over the other. The issue for God's people is how such divided loyalties create moments of disobedience. This means for John Christians are to come out of Babylon in order to avoid participation in her sins as well as to provide an example of what it means to be other than Babylon. Regardless of whether we interpret this passage to refer to Rome or North America or, more appropriately, to both of these, the biblical story is clear that God's people have always struggled with resisting empires in order to be God's city on the hill.

In his attempt to understand the authority that Revelation exercises over Christians in terms of church and state relations (or the dichotomy of traversing multiple cities), William Stringfellow persuasively suggests that if we are to discern the nature of the state biblically then all states, though they are ultimately under the power of God, are nevertheless Babylons.[15] Stringfellow is adamant to point out that the United States, just like every other nation before it and those that will come after it, must be construed biblically. What makes this situation more difficult, and tempting for Christians, is that the United States often claims to be the new Jerusalem, the hope and salvation for the world. Citizens of this particular nation-state imagine themselves to be the chosen people of God not because they are Jewish or have been engrafted into the Jewish story via Christianity, but simply because they are "American." Biblical truths are distorted through this false hermeneutic. Part of what makes this fictitious form of reading the Bible possible, as well as our inability to always see it, is because of what Stringfellow dubs our "naiveté about the Fall."[16] All of creation, though created good, is fallen and in need of redemption. Yet, because of our culture's unfounded optimism in human nature we fail to see how demonic our own projects can become. In terms of the state, Stringfellow suggests that there are, ultimately, only two cities that the Bible narrates: Babylon and Jerusalem:

14. Brook and Gwyther, *Unveiling Empire*, 184.

15. Stringfellow *An Ethic for Christians and Other Aliens in a Strange Land*, 13–17.

16. Ibid., 19.

Babylon is the city of death, Jerusalem is the city of salvation; Babylon, the domination of alienation, babel, slavery, war, Jerusalem, the community of reconciliation, sanity, freedom, peace; Babylon, the harlot, Jerusalem the bride of God; Babylon, the realm of demons and foul spirits, Jerusalem, the dwelling place in which all creatures are fulfilled; Babylon, an abomination to the Lord, Jerusalem, the holy nation; Babylon, doomed, Jerusalem, redeemed.[17]

Stringfellow is suggesting that there are two diametrically opposed cities that constitute creation. This means that any hope in Babylon, or any giving of allegiance to her, her Caesars—party affiliation inconsequential—or her cause is a moment given to the temporal city at the expense of the heavenly city. Stringfellow, echoing the call of St. John, demands that we come out of her, the whore that is Babylon whose imminent destruction will be the cause of celebration in heaven (Revelation 19).

Our presence as Christians must be distinguished from the "Babylonians." The attempt, therefore, to embody what it means to be a people "set apart" from the world is made in order that we can be a light to the world. If we abandon this task we have left the world with no hope as it, as well as the church, must face the judgment of God. The coming judgment, however, need not cause despair. God's judgment entails not only the coming redemption of creation but its present redemption. It is the hope for the future that sustains the very possibility of hope we have in the present. Stringfellow suggests that "hope *now* for human life—hope *now* for nations and principalities—hope *now* for the whole of creation—means the imminence of judgment."[18] The church embodies the very hope that is the history of the entire world, which is, ultimately, a redemptive history. God's judgment is that final moment in this history. It is the moment that Kafka poetically deemed the "day after the last day."[19] It is this day after the last day that Christians are called to embody in order that the world, and all of her rebellious structures and institutions, may too be redeemed.

The kind of politics Christians are called to, therefore, is apocalyptic politics. The word apocalypse refers to an unveiling or a revealing of reality. The general stereotype of apocalyptic language as referring to mass

17. Ibid., 34.

18. Ibid., 15.

19. Kafka, *The Blue Octavo Notebooks*, 28. I am indebted to Dan Burns for this reference.

destruction, fortune-telling prophecy, or acid-based dreams miscon-
strues and obviates its message. An apocalypse is a revelation, and in the
biblical sense it is that moment in which we see the world as it really is.
For Christians, what constitutes the world has been revealed through its
crucifixion of Jesus, and what constitutes the church, and her God, has
been revealed through the resurrection. This is no pie-in-the-sky moment, nor an exercise in mawkish spirituality. When we read of Jesus'
resurrection, our eyes, like those of Paul's on the road to Damascus, are
opened. We understand that what it means to be an apocalyptic people is
to be a people who follow both a crucified and a risen God. Apocalyptic
politics, therefore, is not fulfilled by our tendency to spiritualize the life,
death and resurrection of Jesus any more than they are about, as Yoder
notes, "Russians in Mesopotamia." Apocalyptic politics are "about how
the crucified Jesus is a more adequate key to understanding what God
is about in the real word of empires and armies and markets than is the
ruler in Rome, with all his supporting military, commercial, and sacerdo-
tal networks."[20] Yoder continues,

> The point apocalyptic makes is not only that people who wear
> crowns and who claim to foster justice by the sword are not as
> strong as they think—true claim as that is. . . . It is that people who
> bear crosses are working with the grain of the universe. One does
> not come to that belief by reducing social processes to mechani-
> cal and statistical models, nor by winning some of one's battles for
> the control of one's own corner of the fallen world. One comes to
> it by sharing the life of those who sing about the Resurrection of
> the slain Lamb.[21]

The crucifixion was powers' last-ditch attempt to silence truth, and the
resurrection was the unmasking of its inability to conquer God. These
two events, these divine interruptions in history, re-order history and
demand that Christians live into it.

The apocalypse of Jesus Christ changes everything. It shows us what
to see, what we have not seen, and what we should see.[22] More importantly, it redefines words with fetish-like appeal such as "realism" and
"responsibility." We are now responsible to this apocalyptic order, and
we are being realistic when we live into *it*. This apocalyptic politic is not

20. Yoder, *The Politics of Jesus*, 246.

21. Yoder, "Armaments and Eschatology," 54.

22. Dark, *Everyday Apocalypse*, 10.

an alternative politic, it is the genuine politic by which other politics are measured. It is the politic of the in-breaking kingdom of God. The employment of apocalyptic language reminds us of both the political nature of salvation and its grounding in eschatology. We are a people of the kingdom that is already here, is on the way, and has yet to fully come. As political ambassadors of the city of God we are eschatological witnesses to the way the world was created, was meant to be, and one day will be again. Inasmuch as we embody this politic we embody the life that we are called to exemplify so that others may know the God of all kingdoms. The significant thing about this kind of politic is that it does not demand that we always get "it" right. That is to say, we may look at certain moments of Christian practice as more faithful than others, as we are commanded to practice such discernment, yet remain hopeful due to our inability to control or dictate the future. Neither the future, nor history, is in our hands to determine. We are only to provide a glimpse of God's peaceable kingdom. Though some will remain skeptical of certain tactics employed by those who are attempting to be faithful to this already-here-yet-future politic, we can neither negate nor avoid the politics of Jesus' resurrection. Fortunately, we are free from the tyranny of always getting it right. We are not, however, free from the privilege/burden of revealing Jesus to and for the world. Christians are to embody the politics of the slaughtered Lamb, and though there will be much argument as to what constitutes a faithful witness to this Lamb that there must be a witness is not debatable. Christians are those people who witness to Christ's resurrection and inasmuch as we do this, we betray the apocalyptic content of the Christian politic.

APOPHATIC POLITICS

The anarchist and the Christian have a common origin.

—FRIEDRICH NIETZSCHE

At this point it is necessary to distinguish what makes this a *genuine* politic rather than an *alternative* one, or, even worse, an apolitical or antipolitical politic. In his book *Subversive Orthodoxy*, author Robert Inchausti attempts to reinvigorate the prophetic element that has always been at the core of the church.[23] Inchausti argues that once the church's

---

23. Inchausti, *Subversive Orthodoxy.*

prophetic witness is neglected, lost or abandoned, she becomes an un-mediated vessel for all sorts of misconceptions and ideologies. In a spiri-tualized culture like ours what this has led to is a Christianity that has become content with disembodiment, privatization, and depoliticization. For Inchausti this signals a loss of the one gift the church has to give the world: a prophetic vision of God's kingdom. In order for Inchausti to enable the church to go beyond her own domestication he examines the lives of a variety of Christians—all of whom picture the subversive element of prophecy that lies at the heart of the Gospel. By doing so Inchausti offers a rather convincing case for the possible resuscitation of Christianity through the lives of those who live it well. The power of his argument rests in his ability, not to be theologically innovative but astute at telling the stories of the church's practitioners.

In the third chapter of his book Inchausti examines the lives of several civil discontents such as Martin Luther King, Jr., Dorothy Day, and Thomas Merton. His reasoning for examining their lives in light of a chapter titled "Antipolitical Politics," stems from Vaclav Havel who sug-gests that anti-political politics are a *kind* of politics that does not enact a manipulation of, or a rule over others, but is a process and practice by which the possibility of meaningful lives may be created and sustained.[24] In this sense, Inchausti is right to place the aforementioned Christians in the heart of such a chapter as they all embarked on a mission of creat-ing and sustaining the possibilities for meaningful lives for all persons (rich and poor, oppressor and oppressed). It is undoubtedly the case that people such as Day and King not only refused to underwrite the prevail-ing accounts of political practice but undermined it through their own lives.

Nevertheless, there is a significant problem with the language of anti-political politics. If both Havel and Inchausti presume that one must engage in anti-political or apolitical behavior in order to participate in that good reflective of Christianity, then we must presuppose that politics qua politics assumes an ontology of violence. To presuppose as much is to imagine that the very being of political practice already assumes a fallen state in which participation requires an *accommodation* to the powers and principalities that constitute a post-lapsarian world. In one sense, it is both easy and tempting to agree with this line of thought. In typical two kingdom fashion, either one participates in the kingdom of

24. Inchausti, *Subversive Orthodoxy*, 84.

God or the kingdom of Satan. In the case of the latter, to participate in the political powers that rule this earth is to share in the very kingdoms offered to Jesus by Satan (Luke 4:5–7). Jesus, however, declined to rule over the kingdoms of this earth, and if we are to suggest that true politics stems from the earthly kingdoms then we betray a privileged stance to that temporal space and time known as the secular. Why should our politics be defined by that which Christians are against, or rather, that which is against Christianity? Perhaps it is not the case that politics is the manipulation of others, but temporal politics is the very thing that both Havel and Inchausti rightly critique — these *are* the false politic. Faithful political behavior is not anti-political, for that privileges the orders of the world, but is the only *genuine* politic of which participation in is, for the Christian, mandatory.

Perhaps this seems like a minor point, but I think the remainder of this text will suggest otherwise. For if the world's politics receives a privileged stance then everything that is not of it must be defined as reactionary, rebellious, or anti-political. As Christians we have a very real stake in making sure that we are not defined by what we are against, but what we are for. If Christians believe that true politics stems from participation in God's kingdom then anything less than *this* is reactionary, rebellious, and anti-political. To that end, the people examined in this book are not rebels; it is those who persecute these Christians that are in rebellion. The kind of Christianity I am attempting to narrate, and be narrated by, should, therefore, not be understood as political theology or revolutionary politics. For it is the idea of revolution that is at the core of why it is so often the case that the Christian is not liberated from the powers of the world.

THIS IS NOT A REVOLUTION (NOR AN INSURRECTION)

I would say that the State consists in the codification of a whole number of power relations which render its functioning possible, and that Revolution is a different type of codification of the same relations.

—MICHEL FOUCAULT

In Vernard Eller's book *Christian Anarchy*, he argues that the notion of revolution, an idea so heavily in vogue in the past two centuries, is antithetical to the heart of Christianity. For revolution, as he defines it, is "an all out holy-arky effort to unseat an evil regime (the Establishment) and replace it with a just one (the Revolution)."[25] This is not to suggest that Eller imagines that Christianity should merely accommodate the prevailing order, he is claiming that the very notion of revolution belongs to the realm in which order cannot become anything but disorder. The new power, that which the "revolution" inaugurates, may or may not be as potentially bad as the one it usurped, but it still remains outside of the politics of Jesus. For Eller, Jesus was not a revolutionary as that would have committed him to the kind of antagonistic world in which humans are constantly battling for position. Jesus was no revolutionary for he was not participating in "human-heroic arky power."[26] The Son of God did not come to alter or enhance our current modes of politics. The incarnation displaces not only what we think it means to be political, but the very category of politics itself. For Christians, Jesus does not have a politic nor is representative of one, but as he is fully human and fully divine, Jesus *is* a politic.[27]

Christian anarchism is not a revolutionary politic for it denies the legitimacy of revolution. This is a call for something far more subversive than the replacing of one regime with another. Regime change has been the model of worldly power since its inception. Instead, Christian anarchism rejects the very presuppositions that make the idea of revolution, and, perhaps, even liberation itself, intelligible. Jesus is neither exemplified in Che Guevera or Simon the Zealot.[28] He had no desire to destroy or replace the kingdoms that surrounded him with a different ruler; instead, he established a community of believers who developed and reside in the *altera civitas* on earth: the church. To this end Walter Wink claims that Jesus was not a

> reformer, bringing alternative, better readings of the law. Nor was he a revolutionary, attempting to replace one oppressive power with another (Mark 12:13–17). He went beyond revolution. His struggle was against the basic presuppositions and structures of oppression—against the Domination System itself. Violent revo-

---

25. Eller, *Christian Anarchy*, 74.

26. Ibid.

27. For an extended account of this important point see Yoder's *The Politics of Jesus*.

28. See Cullman, *The State in the New Testament* and Trocme, *Jesus and The Nonviolent Revolution*. Both Cullman and Trocme show how real the option and temptation of embracing the practice of the Zealots was for Jesus.

lution fails because it is not revolutionary enough. It changes the
rulers but not the rules, the ends but not the means.[29]

Wink is suggesting that the act of revolution does not do enough for it
assumes the very apparatus of power that it wishes to overthrow. Jesus,
for Wink, is neither rebel nor reformer because he is neither affirming the
old by striving to reform it or rebel against it; rather, what he introduces
is a soteriological narrative that engrafts its followers into a different
story. This story does not buy into the world's stories but re-narrates all
stories. God's kingdom is not an alternative to worldly powers as it is the
empires, nation-states, and the monarchies that are the alternative(s) to
God's kingdom. Early Christianity recognized this as is apparent in Acts
17 where Paul and his companions were accused by the Thessalonians of
"turning the world upside down" because of their refusal to "honor the
decrees of the emperor, saying that there is another king named Jesus"
(v. 6–7). Their actions were viewed as subversive simply because of their
allegiance to a different king. This king that does not wish to build upon
the old order or introduce something different in its place, as this would
privilege the very apparatus of power in need of redemption. Instead,
Jesus reveals to us God's kingdom that tells a completely different story
than what the world can possibly tell. It is because of this particular
story that the early Christians were viewed as subversive. They were not
subversive because they sought liberation, they were deemed subversive
because their every action was reflective of the kind of king that other
kings must put to death. Ultimately, they introduced a radically different
kind of subversion—one that does not attempt to simply undermine the
system but to *convert* it. The key to such conversion rests not in the ability
to rebel against power, but in the Christian's commitment to pray for it:

> When the Roman archons (magistrates) ordered the early
> Christians to worship the imperial spirit or *genius*, they refused,
> kneeling instead and offering prayers on the emperor's behalf
> to God. This seemingly innocuous act was far more exasperat-
> ing and revolutionary than outright rebellion would have been.
> Rebellion simply acknowledges the absoluteness and ultimacy of
> the emperor's powers and attempts to seize it. Prayer denies that
> ultimacy altogether by acknowledging a higher power. Rebellion
> would have focused solely on the physical institution and its cur-

29. Wink, *The Powers That Be*, 81.

rent incumbents and attempted to displace them by an act of superior force. But prayer challenged the very spirituality of the empire itself and called the empire's "angel," as it were, before the judgment seat of God.[30]

This "seemingly innocuous act," praying for the emperor, posed a major problem for the empire. Armed rebels are easy to demonize and generally pose little problem for any state, at any time, to punish via execution. However, what does one do with a people who are turning the world upside down because they are praying for the very leaders who are demanding total obedience? What does one make of a state that would execute those who are praying for it?

> When Christians knelt in the Colosseum to pray as lions bore down on them, something sullied the audience's thirst for revenge. Even in death these Christians were not only challenging the ultimacy of the emperor and the "spirit" of the empire but also demonstrating the emperor's powerlessness to impose his will even by death. The final sanction had been publicly robbed of its power. Even as the lions lapped the blood of the saints, Caesar was stripped of his arms and led captive in Christ's triumphal procession.[31]

The prayerful and nonviolent response of the followers of Jesus forces Caesar to become a participant in Jesus' victory. The "triumphal procession" of Christ continues through those that follow him as it is in our very "coming out" of our captive cities that we, as a light to the nations, seek their good.

SEEKING THE PEACE OF THE CITY

And should I not be concerned about Nineveh, that great city, in which there are more than a hundred and twenty thousand persons who do not know their right hand from their left, and also many animals?

—JONAH 4:11

To be a people set apart is, as just stated, not an end itself. To be God's people entails the Jeremianic imperative to "seek the peace of the city" of

---

30. Wink, *Naming the Powers*, 110.

31. Ibid., 111.

which God has sent us into exile (Jer 29:7).[32] We are to be an instrument of God's blessings to all nations by bearing witness to the goodness of God. In his book *Mere Discipleship*, Lee Camp argues that it is for this reason alone that Christians are not permitted to

> . . . withdraw themselves from the good of Babylon, but to seek its good—not by adopting the ethics of the Babylonians, not by buying onto the myth that they need to get hold of the mantle of Babylonian imperial power, and not by defeating the Babylonians though revolutionary violence, but by faithful, obedient witness to their God.[33]

The good that Christians are called to embody is intended for all of creation. It is for this reason that it may be said that we must "come out" of Babylon, not in order to withdraw from her, but to stand out from her for her own good. This was the problem in the case of the recalcitrant prophet Jonah who attempted to withdraw from his mission. Jonah's reason for fleeing from his calling to prophesy was not that he thought it was a lost cause, but that he actually believed the Ninevites would hear the word and repent. We are told that not only did the entire city repent, but that the king arose from his throne, disrobed himself and covered his body with sackcloth (Jonah 3:6). Holding the earthly city accountable to God is, as this story suggests, hardly a strategy for withdrawal. In fact, it requires a thoroughgoing engagement with the city. In order to accomplish this, however, the city must be engaged by something other than itself: the church. To seek the city's peace requires the presence of God's people who will not abandon the city. Therefore, to take our task seriously requires that we not gauge ourselves by the world's standards of efficacy or relevance. Following Jeremiah we must observe with John Howard Yoder that "there was never reason for debate about whether that shalom was knowable to the Babylonians, or about whether it was relevant. The need was for the Jewish exiles themselves to believe that that was their mission."[34] The very posture of being exiled, as God's people, is the means by which God calls the earthly cities to God's peace.

For Yoder, the early church understood and adopted this model of existence as vocational. He states that Jesus' impact

---

32. I have written on this passage in my book *The Purple Crown*, 99–120.

33. Camp, *Mere Discipleship*, 83.

34. Yoder, *For the Nations*, 33–34.

. . . in the first century added more and deeper authentically Jewish reasons, and reinforced and further validated the already expressed Jewish reasons, for the already well established ethos of not being in charge and not considering any local state structure to be the primary bearer of the movement of history.[35]

Following the prophetic line of Jeremiah, Jesus solidifies the notion that powerlessness and Diaspora are normative for the elect. Diaspora is a graced and permanent vocation until the heavenly Jerusalem descends upon earth. This demands that we recognize, as Yoder claims was clear in the early church, that "the central meaning of history is borne not by kings and empires but by the church herself."[36] To go into all the nations, drawing disciples from all earthly cities that they may be citizens of the heavenly city, that is the task of the Christian pilgrim.

That Christians are to seek the peace of the city is a staple require-ment of discipleship. The argument, however, centers on *how* one seeks such peace. Christians ranging from Tertullian to St. Augustine, St. Francis to Joan of Arc, and Felix Mantz to Dietrich Bonhoeffer have attempted to practice this command faithfully. All of their paths, as well as ours, may be divergent, but they, and we, share in common this command to seek the peace of our cities. The task is to be able to do so without compromis-ing who we are as Christians. It is my contention that the very moment in which we compromise who we are, we cease seeking the peace of the city. Perhaps no greater temptation to such a compromise stems from the desire, well-intentioned as it may be, to not merely seek the peace of the city but to *secure* it. It is this latter desire that must be overcome, and it is for this reason that I have found it advantageous to examine the Christians in this book as practitioners of Christianity who have waged war well against this temptation. By examining the lives of Dorothy Day and Peter Maurin, Clarence Jordan, and the Berrigan brothers we gain a sense of what it means to be an exilic people called to seek the good of the temporal cities without attempting to secure it. That these people were all mocked, ostracized, belittled, as well as fined and arrested should come as no surprise since Christian history reveals to us that such things are going to occur. From the prophets to the disciples, the biblical witness is clear that to conform one's will to the will of God is going to necessitate,

---

35. Ibid., 69.

36. Yoder, *The Christian Witness to the State*, 16–17.

so claims Jesus, resistance and persecution (John 15:19-20). That our participation in the kingdom of God entails rejection by so many is often the very sign that we are on the right path.

German pastor and theologian Dietrich Bonhoeffer said that "Christianity without discipleship is always Christianity without Christ" and the lives of those listed in this book are but a few that provide a wonderful model for what it means to practice Christianity.[37] Their following of Christ makes them participants in the divine economy that is the triune God. Such participation, as Graham Ward notes, leads to beatification—or, true citizenship.[38] Beatification, the process of being made participants in God's economy, is the performance of our heavenly citizenship. Peter claims that through the promises made by God we are able to escape the corruption that is all that is in rebellion against God in order that we "may become participants of the divine nature" (2 Pet 1:4). We are beatified through our participation in God's nature as exemplified in the practice of responsible heavenly citizenship. Of course, in order to enact this citizenry one assumes a loyalty to the city of God as revealed in the church on earth. It is for this reason that the church is not simply one society among or within a plethora of contending societies; instead, the church may best be understood as a polis, or, as *the* polis.[39] It is within the church that the participant is trained for what it means to be a citizen of the heavenly Jerusalem as well as a citizen for the world. At the same time, however, the church is not a polis if by this we assume a fixed space secured by the efforts of Christians. Such an account would undermine the kind of posture I think Christians are called to embody. Rather, the church is a culture, a society, a politic, and an ethic that does not necessarily occupy a space as much as it endures through time. John Milbank argues that the church transforms space in such a way that it defies that idea of a fixed "space." This makes the city of God an impossible possibility. It is a nomadic city that is without walls or gates. It is unlike any other polis, city or established geographical space. It defies our canonization of thought in terms of what we think a city is and converts us to a different

37. Bonhoeffer, *The Cost of Discipleship*, 63–64.

38. Ward, "Why is the City so Important for Christian Theology?"

39. Though of course it should be noted that the church is not simply a specimen of the broader category of "polis." On this point see Arne Rassmusson, *The Church as Polis*.

understanding of space altogether. Milbank argues that whatever kind of space it is that the church can be said to occupy it is

> . . . not, like Rome, an asylum constituted by the 'protection' of-fered by a dominating class over a dominated, in the face of an external enemy. This form of refuge is, in fact, but a dim archetype of the real refuge provided by the Church, which is the forgiveness of sins. Instead of a 'peace' achieved through the abandonment of the losers, the subordination of potential rivals and resistance to enemies, the Church provides a genuine peace by its memory of all victims, its equal concern for all its citizens and its self-ex-posed offering of reconciliation to enemies. The peace within the city walls opposing the 'chaos' without, is, in fact, no peace at all compared with a peace coterminous with all Being whatsoever. *Space is revolutionized: it can no longer be defended, and even the barbarians can only respect the sanctuary of the Basilica.*[40]

The city of God manifest as the church on earth revolutionizes space by enduring through others' space. The kind of citizen it produces, there-fore, is the kind that exists as an exiled pilgrim from her true home who, nevertheless, seeks the welfare of those that surround her. This is the gift that God gives to the world: to provide the world with a witness to the true God and God's true city (Matt 24:14). This gift can only come in the form of her inhabitants, and it is to them that we now turn.

---

40. Milbank, *Theology and Social Theory*, 392. (Italics mine.)

3 Catholic Workers Unite!

So, friends, every day do something that won't compute. Love the Lord. Love the world. Work for nothing. Take all that you have and be poor. Love someone who does not deserve it.

—WENDELL BERRY

The vast majority of anarchists, historically speaking, share one thing in common: the protest of profit-driven capitalism.[1] Though the protest of capitalism has, in recent years, taken on a rather fetish-like life form (marketable, packaged, and sold to non-capitalists) it nevertheless remains true that capitalism, whether you like it or not, is an all-encompassing way of life. It appears that all of creation is reducible to the market. We buy, use, discard, and buy again. Everything from clothes to religion, food to ideas, entertainment to spouses—it is all for sale. The oldies song "You Better Shop Around" was referring to potential lovers, not good vegetables. Protesting capitalism even serves this comprehensive sociopolitic as the number of anti-capitalist books, tracts, music, films, t-shirts and bumper stickers still require one thing in order to be seen, read, or heard: they must be purchased. The protest of capitalism itself does little more than buttress the very thing being called into question. Capitalism is omnipotent.

The more well-known protests of capitalism from within anarchist circles stem from writers such as Proudhon, Bakunin, and Kroptokin. All three of these thinkers were greatly concerned with the converting of

1. This excludes the rather anomalous group of anarchists referred to as anarcho-capitalists. Capitalism has, since its inception, undergone a vast number of definitions which accounts for some of the ambiguity of certain anarchical postures towards capitalism. In the nineteenth century capitalism was often defined simply as the state of maintaining capital, or holding goods, whereas by the twentieth century it came to mean a more specific form of accruing goods as determined by private beneficiaries that was not regulated by the state but by the free market.

money into capital as something that can become productive in and of itself. Their central point of contention was aimed at how the necessity to profit requires the "voluntary" labor of the masses for the benefit of the few. Neither money nor property can produce anything on its own so capitalism requires the labor of someone else to convert it into a profit that can only be a profit if the labor required to produce it is underpaid. One might say, with Proudhon, that what profit actually represents is unpaid labor.[2]

The church has also produced her fair share of critics of capitalism. In an effort to not reproduce those arguments here, it is enough to simply note that many recent ecclesial critics voice their opposition against two major tenets embedded within the capitalism: usury and greed.[3] Usury was forbidden by biblical Judaism and its prohibition was assumed by both the early and medieval church. The practice of usury, until the late sixteenth century, was understood by many Christians to be a faithless practice. In a spirit similar to the aforementioned anarchists, money does not produce money, nor should one lend it with the expectation of receiving back more than was loaned. Given that Jesus told his followers that if someone asks you for something you should give it to them (Matt 5:42), the idea that you could loan someone money and reap back more than what you loaned was a scandal destined to send the loaner to Dante's fourth level of hell.

The sin of greed is also a necessity in a capitalist order. Even though we are always promised costumer satisfaction, such a state of being is actually prohibited. If one were to become fulfilled, then they would become an obstacle to the ends of this culture. Capitalism thrives on short-term commitments. In order to do our job of buttressing this economy we the consumers must do exactly that for which we are named: consume. If we do not purchase new cars every four years then the economy plummets. If we do not grow tired of our clothes quick enough, then the economy plummets. If we become satisfied with what we already have we become a threat to the very survival of our neighbors. One must be a materialist if they are going to be a responsible capitalist. Spending money is an altruistic enterprise. Nothing is more telling of this than George Bush's immediate response to the destruction of the Twin Towers on September

2. Proudhon, *What is Property?* 148–51.

3. For an extended critique of capitalism, as well as an engagement with a large variety of voices both for and against it, see D. Stephen Long's *Divine Economy.*

11, 2001 when he told those whom he represents to "go shopping." As shallow and as superficial as that may sound, it was a good and necessary command for the wellbeing of this republic. Shopping is a moral obligation for each citizen of this culture. To refuse to shop spells doom for the sacred American way of life. Greed is a virtue, and hell is now reserved for those who would share their goods.

We have certainly come a long way since the writing of Dante. Problems of avarice or usury are no longer an issue. We are simply told not to want *too much* stuff. The ban on usury and greed is simply no longer viable or reasonable and can be set aside as a silly legalistic mode of thinking belonging to an unenlightened age. There is no going back. As problematic as capitalism is, as much as some of us may wish to resist it, we have to contend with the fact that we are all capitalists. It has become our fate. We own goods, we purchase goods, we sell goods, and we have become goods. The good of this economy is to turn everything into a commodity. It is especially good to make as much profit as possible as that enables us to spend more money for the good of this economy. Despite Jesus' and the prophets' continual demand to not only share resources but to give them away, as capitalists we simply have to co-opt our Christianity for a more realistic one. Jesus' command to the rich man to give away all of his goods, or even half of them, must be interpreted through the lens of our economy which negates any hermeneutic that would have us to take Jesus seriously. Jesus' declaration of Jubilee, the forbiddance of any kind of monopolization of land or goods, is, thanks to the Constitution, not realistic. We now have to imagine, we are told, that in terms of his politics of money, Jesus must have meant something else.

Unfortunately, much of why the continual protests of capitalism, of which there is no short supply, continues to fall on deaf ears is that there are few visible alternatives for what a life lived counter to capitalism would look like. Those few, however, have provided a powerful counter-testimony to what it means to embody Jesus' divine economy. Eberhard Arnold and the Bruderhof, the Hutterites, the Amish, as well as numerous Christian intentional communities of the twentieth century, have all provided glimpses of how to escape a life of consumer condemnation. Odds are, however, few of us are going to become Amish. Perhaps we should. There are, of course, other witnesses that allow us to see how we can participate in a different kind of economy. One group in particular, the Catholic Worker movement, has performed this task exceedingly well. By focusing on the Catholic Worker I will examine how their witness calls into question basic "common sense" assumptions Christians make about money and property, and how this alters our perceptions about the co-opting of capitalism with Christianity.

DOROTHY AND PETER

Anarchism means "Love God and do as you will!"

—DOROTHY DAY

In 1973 Dorothy Day was arrested and jailed for taking part in a banned picketing line supporting the rights of farm workers. She was 75 years old. This was not the first time Dorothy had been arrested, though it would be her last. During the course of her life she was not only arrested multiple times, but she was interrogated by the FBI, disowned by certain ecclesial officials, and even, literally, dodged bullets. What I find to be most significant about the various interrogations, death-threats, charges of sedition, diverse forms of ecclesial reprimand, and repeated arrests, especially her last one, was the fact that practitioners of law and order felt obliged, once again, to arrest this elderly Catholic pacifist. This, I think, continues to speak volumes about what it means to follow Jesus in our freedom loving, religiously obsessed culture.

Day was born on November 8, 1897 in Brooklyn, New York. Her family relocated to Berkeley, then Oakland, and, finally, Chicago. Though she was baptized in an Episcopalian church, she rejected her religious faith during college and discovered faith in more radical movements associated with communism, anarchism, and socialism. Day gravitated toward anything that offered some sort of hope against the systemic oppression of the poor. She wrote for various radical journals, magazines, and newspapers, many of which rightly accused Christianity of perpetuating the sexist, classist, and racist culture indicative of the early twentieth century. Day was seeking a way in the world that would enable her to help alleviate much of the misery she was witnessing. She desperately wanted to change not just the conditions that create inequality but the very formations that render such conditions possible—if not inevitable. She was surrounded by rampant poverty, class war, militarism, bigotry toward minorities and women, and this was all perpetuated and sustained by a nation primarily consisting of Christians.

Though she spent the majority of her formative years surrounded by close friends who were antagonistic toward the church, she continually felt as though there was something within Christianity that could, if tried, offer a response to the sufferings and chaos of her culture. Day, however, despised the apparent hypocrisy of those who called themselves Christian, and so a faith-based response was hardly an option. In many ways, this is exactly what drove her to find community with more self-sacrificial secular radicals because when it came to Christians she said, "I did not see anyone taking off their coat and giving it to the poor. I didn't see anyone having a banquet and calling in the lame, the halt, and the blind."[4] She noticed that the majority of churchgoers either had enough money so as not to have to bother about the harsh realities of the world or "smiled at and fawned upon" the rich in hopes of attaining their level of success. Concern for the poor and downtrodden, and especially the circumstances that led to poverty, seemed to be the furthest thing from the Christian's mind. She could not understand such Christian indifference as she, though not a Christian—yet with great Christian sensibilities—thought that every home should "be open to the lame, the halt and the blind" and that it was only "then did people really live, really love their brothers. In such love was the abundant life and I did not have the slightest idea how to find it."[5] Though she often felt haunted by God, and even attempted to turn to God on various occasions, it was not until her late twenties that she would undergo the conversion that turned her into what many have claimed to be "the most influential, interesting, and significant figure" in the history of American Catholicism.[6]

In 1926, while living on Staten Island in a deeply committed relationship with fellow anarchist Forster Batterham, Dorothy became pregnant. This was not her first pregnancy, though this one would be different (as her first ended in an abortion). During her second pregnancy she began frequenting a local Catholic Church. She enjoyed what appeared to be a kind of spiritual contentment from many of the practitioners as well as a new sense of what it may mean to be one who follows Jesus. After her

4. Day, *The Long Loneliness*, 39.

5. Ibid.

6. Ellsberg, *All Saints*, 519.

child was born, she decided that her daughter Tamar Teresa, against the wishes of Forster, would be baptized. Dorothy eventually followed Tamar into Catholicism resulting in the dissolution of her common law marriage. Forster, a man she deeply loved, left because she chose the church over their relationship. Once he departed, she too left their cottage and moved back to the city. This move proved to be significant as she came into contact with a French man often referred to as the St. Francis of the twentieth century: Peter Maurin.

In December of 1932, she met Peter who had been waiting for her return from a Hunger March in Washington, DC. Dorothy was attempting to come to terms with how far she felt her life was from the concrete issues that cause suffering for others. While she was in the capitol she visited a church in order to pray that a more meaningful approach to the integration of Christian faith and social issues might come to light.[7] She said that for

> ... seven years I had been a Catholic. My brother and sister-in-law at that time were Communists. My friends were Communists or fellow travelers, and I didn't know any Catholics except the parish priest to whom I never spoke outside of the confessional. I read Karl Adam, St. John of the Cross, St. Teresa of Avila, St. Augustine and the *Imitation of Christ*. I knew of the social teachings of the Church, but I felt that eternal life was more important than this present life, and besides, I was enjoying the present life. I was a convert Catholic; I could no longer work with the Communist party as I had years before. The last job I had had with them was working for the Anti-Imperialist League, which was calling attention to American Aggression in Nicaragua. But I knew no work I could do within the framework of the Church. I had done newspaper work, writing articles, doing research, covering labor conflicts, working long hours for small wages as a Catholic. It was solitary work.[8]

She was not clear on what it meant to be a Catholic and yet still be involved in the ongoing struggle against those things that led to the oppression of others. Nevertheless, despite her work she started to grow, hesitantly, satisfied with digging roots—that is, with becoming comfortable with where she was in the world. Yet, when she arrived back in New York,

7. Day and Sicius, *Peter Maurin*, 37.
8. Ibid., 38.

Peter, who had been directed by the editor of *Commonweal* magazine to find Dorothy, was there waiting. He was a Godsend, she claimed, as he "came to be my teacher, to disturb my content, to remind me that we are pilgrims, and that we have no right to dig our roots in."[9]

Peter was born on May 9, 1877 in a small community in southern France. His mother died after giving birth to five children, of which only three survived. His father remarried and his stepmother gave birth to eighteen children. His brothers and sisters consisted of teachers, carpenters, farmhands, monks, and nuns. Peter worked various odd jobs, as he would do his whole life, and spent a significant amount of time wandering France working as a cocoa salesman. At one point he became involved with a Christian democratic political movement known as Le Sillion, and eventually made his way to Canada in the hopes of settling on some land. From there he moved to the states where he worked in brickyards, on farms, in steel mills and various other jobs requiring both skilled and unskilled labor. He finally settled in New York and became a French tutor. Peter refused to charge for his lessons and relied upon the generosity of his students to see that he did not starve. By the time he met Dorothy Day he was already fifty-five.[10] She claimed that it was amazing how little they understood each other at first.[11]

This was understandable given the large gulf that existed between the two in terms of their histories. He was from France while she was born in the states. Not only was he more than twenty years older than her, he was a peasant while she had only known the city. His thoughts on work revolved around agriculture and the good of working with one's hands, while her thoughts on worked centered around machines and factories and the kind of alienation produced by these conditions. He spoke incessantly, to the chagrin of some; she spoke through her writing.

What they did share in common was Catholicism. Dorothy was a relatively recent convert while Peter had spent much of his life reading and studying the patrisitics, medieval theology, and Catholic social thought. He had profound respect for both the authority and the tradition of premodern theology, and though he never desired a return to this period he did think that it held the resources possible to overcome the alienation

---

9. Ibid.

10. For more details of his early years see Day and Sicius, *Peter Maurin*, 1–27 and Ellis, *Peter Maurin*, 21–30.

11. Day, *The Long Loneliness*, 175.

that modernity imparted on the present social order. Peter's ideas did not center on innovation or new ways of thinking, rather what made him so subversive was his return to tradition. It was this tradition that he imparted upon Dorothy making possible the grassroots movement known as the Catholic Worker.

THE CATHOLIC WORKER MOVEMENT

The Sermon on the Mount is our Christian manifesto.

—DOROTHY DAY

Peter taught the need for a "green revolution" that would enable others to know who it is they are called to be. His thought centered on personalism: the idea that what is truly real, what is ontological, is the person, and that the measure of any good institution was its ability to enable the individual person the space needed to recognize their purpose. This personalist revolution would be underwritten by a theology of simplicity, decentralization, the sharing of goods, nonviolence, prayer, the Eucharist, and a return to the land. The bulk of his theology was often scribbled on little sheets of paper that he would pass out or real aloud, over and over again, to anyone who would listen. He once even booked himself as a comedian at the infamous Apollo theatre in Harlem in order to read his "easy essays." Though there is something truly comedic in such a performance, the stunned and perturbed crowd quickly demanded his exit. Much of the themes that would narrate the direction the Catholic Worker would take are prominent in his essay showcasing his respect of medieval Irish monasticism:

> When the Irish scholars
>
> decided to lay the foundations
>
> of medieval Europe,
>
> they established:
>
> Centers of Thought
>
> in all the cities of Europe
>
> as far as Constantinople,
>
> where people

could look for thought

so they could have light.

Houses of Hospitality

where Christian charity

was exemplified.

Agricultural Centers

where they combined

(a) Cult—that is to say Liturgy

(b) with Culture—that is to say Literature

(c) with Cultivation—that is to say Agriculture.[12]

By returning to the tradition of Catholicism, Peter and Dorothy established a three-fold program that included roundtable discussions, the development of houses of hospitality, and agronomic universities.[13] This would be the basis, along with their newspaper, *The Catholic Worker*, for the movement they created.

First, roundtable discussions were necessary in order to allow space for the clarification of thought. The scholar and the worker were to become one. The genius of this move was the refusal to separate the good of both the mind and the body. They wanted all who participated in this movement to work with both their hands and their heads. This also called into question the lines between all too easy distinctions between theory and practice. One's practice would lead to theories while one's theories would lead to different practices. Which precedes the other is neither clear, nor necessary epistemological knowledge. Practice is embodied theory and theory is the explication of practice. These discussions would be informed by the present work at hand while also attempting to discover how certain ills could be remedied. Folks ranging from a variety of different backgrounds, whether race, sex, or class would contribute by participating in argumentative sessions whose goal was to create an ideal vision of what it was that they were attempting to achieve. It is during this part of the program that participants would discover where they were, where they ought to be, and how they would get there.

12. Maurin, *Easy Essays*, 142.

13. Ibid., 36–37.

Secondly, they created houses of hospitality. Again, they were not attempting to do anything new, but simply appealed to an old canon law that required churches to provide shelter for those who needed it. This appeal fell on many deaf ears, yet did not deter them from fulfilling their duty as good Catholics. Due to the onslaught of the Depression, which deprived millions of their homes and ability to procure food, the Catholic Worker demanded that Jesus' call to feed the hungry and clothe the naked be taken literally. There was no debate as to how or when this was to occur, it was just a matter of people needing food and those with it sharing it. They immediately rented a small apartment and began a bread and soup line.

These houses of hospitality, however, were not simply for the poor and downtrodden. Their purpose was twofold: First, they would provide food and shelter for those who lacked it, and secondly, these houses would provide the opportunity for those who had such goods the ability to share them. Those who shared their goods were able to participate in an economy that claims goods are only good if they are shared goods. This was more than rosy sentiment; this was, for the Catholic Worker, the very process of salvation. By the sharing of one's resources the Christian is fulfilling Christ's command to love one another. By being receptive to the gift of giving, the one in need finds oneself intertwined in a gift-exchange economy predicated on the One who gave everything for his creation.[14] It is precisely because of the giving of everything by Jesus, his goods, his forsaking of temporal power, his life, which makes sense of the Catholic Worker's own form of life. Dorothy, Peter, and other eventual participants, lived in these houses of hospitality. They worked, reared families, and shared space within the very environment that attracted Jesus. Participants in the Catholic Worker Movement were poor like Jesus, loved their enemies as Jesus loved his enemies, and sacrificed many comforts most of us assume to be necessities.

Finally, Peter imagined that a return to the land, in the form of self-sustenance, was the answer to an industrial economy that, he thought, necessitated recurring unemployment, the notion of work as a commodity and the rigorous maintenance of a class system.[15] By looking to the

14. For a more detail account of the theological ethics of a gift-exchange economy see Long and York, "Remembering: Offering our Gifts" in Wells and Hauerwas, *Blackwell Companion to Christian Ethics*, 332–45.

15. Maurin, *Easy Essays*, 93–101.

land people would be taught how to build their own houses, raise their own food, and create a life in which work was understood as a gift given for the good of the community rather than as a commodity owned and, subsequently, discarded. The purpose of developing farming communes was to strip work of the notion that it should be concerned with profit when what was required was an emphasis upon need of others. For Peter, the notion of work as a practice of turning profit subverted the meaning of work and turned it into a job.[16] Jobs serve the very structure that alienates one from the notion that there can be a common good in which one can place their service. Jobs serve to buttress a factory-based system in which both humans and their objects of creation are reduced to commodities that are only good inasmuch as they can aid in the production of profit for the few elite. Work, on the other hand, serves a common good, a common end, and a shared vision of the chief end of humanity. The Catholic Worker exists not only to serve the needy, but to provide a vision of the peaceable kingdom. This is a glimpse in which the Catholic Worker Houses of Hospitality show the world the God it is worshipping and how this God responds to those in need. It thus extends the invitation to any who would like to participate in this here and now, and yet-to-be kingdom as a soteriological alternative to the politics of the world. The implementation their vision, and its ongoing life that consists of almost 200 Catholic Worker communities in the United States, creates a space where the various politics of this world are called into question. In this respect, the obtaining of food, shelter and clothing, the roundtable discussions in which every voice, especially the "least of these," counts, and the life together on the farm communes are issues related to soteriology. Their threefold plan, underwritten by the liturgy of the church, is an act of discipleship in which the everyday attempt at survival becomes a conscientious decision as to whether or not to follow Jesus. Participation in such a life as this, with its concomitant emphasis on worship and the practice of nonviolence, offers the world a different way of dealing with enemies, with strangers, with the other. To be exact, the Catholic Worker Movement actually calls into question the very category of the "other" inasmuch as they have insisted on practicing solidarity with the other, on being *with* them to such a degree that they are truly *one*. This is, perhaps, the most scandalous aspect of the Catholic Worker Movement. It is their

16. Maurin, *Easy Essays*, 91.

willingness to become poor for the poor, and the very idea that Christians should, minimally, entertain the possibility of voluntary poverty for the sake of discipleship that proves to be a considerable thorn in the flesh for mainstream Christianity. To understand why voluntary poverty may be a necessary practice for those of us disciplined by a capitalist consumer politic demands questions regarding what it means to be a Christian in an affluent culture whose chief goal is that of obtaining insatiable wealth. When the common good has been reduced to creating a politic in which the only good is the securing of more and more private goods, what possible sort of response can a Christian give that might call into question the very nature of this so-called good? To understand the response of the Catholic Worker is to understand why their path of discipleship is not a very well worn one. To understand their path, however, one must understand their account of money.

ENDORSING LEGALIZED ROBBERY

Much more seriously than they themselves realize, property is (the bourgeoisie's) God, their only God, which long ago replaced in their hearts the heavenly God of the Christians. And, like the latter in the days of yore, the bourgeois are capable of suffering martyrdom and death for the sake of this God. The ruthless and desperate war they wage for the defense of property is not only a war of interests: it is a religious war in the full meaning of the word.

—MIKHAIL BAKUNIN

The French anarchist/socialist Pierre Joseph Proudhon notoriously claimed that "property is theft."[17] Proudhon meant many things by this statement chiefly that the sovereign right of property leads to the monopolization of earth's resources as held by corporations, governments or individuals. By what claims and under what authority can the earth's resources be said to belong to any one person or people? The very instituting of property—of something *belonging* to someone is a mischievous trick that originates, at some point, in conquest. In terms of private property what Proudhon is referring to is the private ownership of productive property, not personal possessions. Anarchists worry about how the relegating of ownership of productive goods results in the enslaving of

---

17. Proudhon, *What is Property*, 11.

humans to mine these goods for the profit of the owners. The resources of the earth should be for all creatures, not just for the few fortunate. Theft occurs when governments legalize the exploitation and monopolization of necessary "products" for all people by placing them in the hands of the very few whose sole purpose is to profit off of other's needs.

For Christians, though such a critique as leveled by anarchists should be taken seriously, theft can occur in other ways as well. In terms of personal possessions, neither Maurin nor Day were strictly against having them. Though in practice they had very little of anything that can be said to be privately owned, they simply imagined that in order for goods to be good they would have to be shared goods. The question for Christians is how does the personal ownership of goods come at the expense of those without need? As an example, how can Christians justify having savings accounts while millions go without food or shelter? Or, how can Christians accrue more and more clothing while so many go cold in the streets? These are basic questions asked by the Catholic Worker and they are not, by any means, new questions. St. John Chrysostom, archbishop of Constantinople in the late fourth and early fifth centuries, claimed that the idea of private property, regardless of how lawful it may be, is not of Christian inspiration.[18] Chrysostom's thoughts are similar to Proudhon's as Chrysostom preached that one's goods "are not his own, but belong to his fellow servants." Chrysostom, however, takes it to another level by claiming that anything a person has that goes beyond what the necessity of life requires is stealing from the poor.[19] This is a radical redefining of what constitutes theft. The notion that God is the creator of all, and that all things are here for the nourishment of all creatures, forces us to rethink what it means to practice the ownership of personal possessions. This is not to say we cannot have things, but it does demand that we examine how owning things may or may not come at the expense of those who lack the basic necessities of life. To quote a contemporary of Chrysostom, St. Ambrose: "It is the hungry man's bread that you withhold, the naked man's cloak that you store away, the money that you bury in the earth is the price of the poor man's ransom and freedom."[20]

---

18. Chrysostom, *On Wealth and Poverty*, 13.

19. Ibid., 13.

20. Aquinas, *Summa Theologica*, II–II, Q 66, article 7.

Though it may be "common sense" to many of us as to what is and is not stealing, according to the early church, and throughout the middle ages, having a surplus of goods while others are in need makes us, literally, thieves. In what could be described as a sort of "Robin Hood" ethic, St. Thomas Aquinas argued that if a person is in serious need and another has excessive goods then it is permissible for the one in need to take whatever is required in order to survive:

> [I]f the need be so manifest and urgent, that it is evident that the present need must be remedied by whatever means be at hand . . . then it is lawful for a man to succor his own need by means of another's property, by taking it either openly or secretly: nor is this properly speaking theft or robbery.[21]

The one who takes out of dire need from those with excess is not committing theft, rather the one who holds excessive goods while others go without are the thieves. This is a unique interpretation of the commandment "thou shall not steal." But its interpretation by pre-modern Christianity goes against the common currency that would suggest the commandments can be understood as some sort of universal ethic. For Aquinas, and much of the patristic and medieval tradition, the idea that one can know the good abstracted from the worship of God was not possible. So even in terms of something like theft we can never be too sure that we can even know what stealing is outside correct worship of God. It is only by participating in the narrative traditions of Israel and the church that Christians come to know the purpose of goods as well as what constitutes theft. The church considers actions such as murder, lying, or theft within a different framework from those who operate under a different narrative. What passes for legal ownership in the modern world could be robbery in terms of Christian thought.

These resources were very much at hand for Peter who exposed Dorothy to what he considered an appropriate Catholic indoctrination. Though neither one ever suggested stealing from the rich in order to give to the poor, they did operate within this thoroughly historical Christian conception of the purpose of goods. Christians, by being Christian, must hold a different account of the appropriate ends of goods. There should be no one going hungry as there is more than enough resources to share with all. By establishing the Catholic Worker, Peter and Dorothy were

21. Ibid.

attempting to hold the Catholic Church accountable to her own best self. As Dorothy once said, it was not how the church was behaving that attracted her to it; it was what the church was supposed to be that led her to her conversion. They attempted to hold the church accountable to its own best tradition and push it to take seriously that to which some of its greatest practitioners have known to be true. The Catholic Worker stressed a disciplined reconfiguration of how Christians must live given that they are surrounded by an economy that is in direct opposition to the way of Jesus. Peter argued that this reconfiguration not only required a thorough knowledge of church history, it also demanded that we learn how to see within the poor the goodness of God. Those of us who have been inundated under the banner of providential material blessings as a sign of God's favor may find nothing more difficult than discovering God in the poor. Maurin claimed it was a necessity for one's salvation. In his essay *We Seem to Think* he wrote:

> St. Francis thought
>
> that to choose to be poor
>
> is just as good
>
> as if one should marry
>
> the most beautiful girl in the world.
>
> We seem to think
>
> that poor people
>
> are social nuisances
>
> and not the Ambassadors of God.
>
> We seem to think
>
> that Lady Poverty
>
> is an ugly girl
>
> and not the beautiful girl
>
> that St. Francis of Assisi
>
> says she is.
>
> And because we think so,
>
> we refuse to feed the poor
>
> with our superfluous goods

and let the politicians

feed the poor

by going around

like pickpockets,

robbing Peter,

to pay Paul,

and feeding the poor

by soaking the rich.[22]

Peter fell in love with Lady Poverty, not in order to romanticize poverty as in end in itself, but in order to call into question the reasons why many Christians in North America find it difficult to have any convictions that might make them poor. It simply was not enough to help the person on the street; you had to become the person on the street. Peter was a tireless worker who worked long days of rough labor, preached on every street corner he could find, and gave away whatever was asked of him. Because of this, he lived in poverty. Dorothy claimed that during his life he had been insulted countless times, mostly by other Christians, and that he suffered many ridiculous mishaps due to his "poor" appearance:

> He had been taken for a plumber and left to sit in the basement when he had been invited to dinner. He had been thrown out of a Knights of Columbus meeting. One pastor who invited him to speak demanded the money back which he had sent Peter for carfare to his upstate parish, because, he said, we had sent him a Bowery bum, and not the speaker he expected.[23]

The idea of a man of God being mistaken for a homeless "bum," though not in any way a stretch of the biblical imagination, appears to have been as much of an affront in the early part of the twentieth century as it is now. Christians, if truly blessed by God, it appears, wear their blessings, drive their blessings, and live in blessings. A quick perusal of most popular Christian literature seems to suggest that "blessings" are synonymous with material gain, and one thing that Maurin lacked was material gain. However, this may have been one of the reasons Day claimed "he was

---

22. Maurin, *Easy Essays*, 123–24.
23. Day, *The Long Loneliness*, 280.

. . . holier than anyone we ever knew."[24] He was holy not because he was poor; rather, he was poor because he was holy.

Kelly Johnson states it well when she says that "Maurin was not original. He was profoundly traditional, and in twentieth-century America, that meant he was radical."[25] They were leaning on their tradition in order to understand what it means to be with those poor that Jesus said would always be with us (Mark 14:7). One of their chief influences for how to engage problems associated with forced poverty in the twentieth-century, and what this means for how Christians should understand the purpose of goods, came from a thirteenth-century monk who was fond of enlisting all creatures in the path of Jesus, even birds.

JUST BEGGING TO BE GOOD

True prayer does not consist in asking favors from a king-God, but in giving alms to a beggar-God.

—GUSTAVE THIBON

Prior to his conversion Giovanni di Bernardone lived what might be considered a relatively normal life. He was schooled in the finer things as was customary of a prosperous family. He wrote poetry, wore expensive clothing, surrounded himself with wealthy friends and, when necessary, engaged in the occasional street fight. He joined the military and, after surviving being taken hostage in a skirmish, eventually moved back home to resume his normal activities. His earliest biographer, Thomas of Celano, claims that Bernardone was raised like all other children, that is, "in accordance of the vanity of the world."[26] Vanity, pridefulness, the search for wealth, the love of all things temporal, it is these practices that plague those who are called "Christian in name, and this pernicious teaching has become so established and prescribed, as though by public law, that people seek to educate their children from the cradle on very negligently and dissolutely."[27] Thomas of Celano's criticism was targeted at his culture in which practices such as self-indulgence, greed, and the

24. Ibid., 281.
25. Kelly Johnson, *The Fear of Beggars*, 184.
26. Thomas of Celano, *St. Francis of Assisi*, 5.
27. Ibid.

accumulation of both wealth and status were assumed to be necessary habits taught and learned in order for the average child to succeed. If Celano were describing and calling into question our contemporary culture we would hardly be shocked. Instead, Celano was critiquing thirteenth century Christendom and attempting to narrate how the behavior of Giovanni di Bernardone, the eventual St. Francis of Assisi, undermined the very culture in which he lived. St. Francis, as is well known, shunned his life of affluence, gave away all of his goods, rejected the practice of violence, befriended all creatures (from crickets to wolves) and, like a good monk, married poverty. Each one of these practices—the sharing of goods, the refusal to learn war, affirming the goodness of all creatures as manifestations of God's wisdom—are as much, if not more so, at odds with our world today as they were in the thirteenth century. It is for this very reason that Peter, who many consider to be the St. Francis of the twentieth century, demanded that we embrace "not a new philosophy but a very old philosophy, a philosophy so old it looks new."[28]

Parts of Peter's intentions were to retrieve the Thomistic doctrine of the common good. This is not to say that he thought that Christian ethics could or should be utilized for non-Christians, but that the *telos* of all humans resides in the eventual hoped-for union with the triune God. The well-being of all creatures is intertwined and interdependent with all others as all have their end in friendship with God. The good of the individual is inextricably bound to the good of others as friendship with God is only possible through friendship with one another (1 John 4:20). Capitalism severs these connections in order to reduce all of life to mere consumption. What constitutes friendship is no longer the shared pursuit of union with God, but stems from class and the ability to spend and consume. Any common good or purpose other than that of being able to autonomously follow one's own desires, as dictated by the market, is difficult to discern, and inevitably requires that Christianity become privatized and self-serving. The Catholic Worker invites us into a different order, one not predicated upon a narrative of rights, property, and self-sufficiency, but one of sharing, humility, and, perhaps, the practice of begging as a possible remedy for the tyranny of love of self.

Peter imagined that a recovery of the Christian vocation of voluntary poverty, accompanied by begging, was necessary for Christians to be able

---

28. Maurin, *Easy Essays*, 93.

to see the God of the poor. Voluntary poverty has a rich history in the church and has mostly been associated with the religious (e.g., monks, nuns or priests). The giving away of all goods in an effort to follow Jesus in one's concern for the "least of these" has carried with it high esteem from the church hierarchy even though it s rarely practiced. What attracted both Peter and Dorothy to Francis was his ability to locate Christian virtue within the act of begging. Begging strips the beggar of the pride that accompanies self-sufficiency. Today one of our greatest concerns is that we will become a burden on our family, so we place our parents and our handicapped in homes in order to free us from their claims and to free them from having to claim us. Francis could not have imagined a greater sin. The longing for complete autonomy, from freedom of dependency, is contrary to the very image of which we are created. Being created in the image of the triune God requires that we participate in the sociality of our created natures. For Francis, begging reminds us how intertwined and interdependent we are on one another. But it does more than this. It becomes part of the story of salvation because it not only rescues us from pride, but affords others the opportunity to care one another. Begging is a form of gift-exchange that turns our eyes and our bodies back to the gift given by Jesus. As Jesus emptied himself for the sake of the world, we too empty ourselves. We become completely dispossessed so that we may become possessed by only God. Though we may not all be called to begging, we are called to gift-giving, and the witness of a Francis of Assisi or a Peter Maurin demands that we call into question our initial reactions to beggars.

For many people there are no greater feelings of uneasiness that occur when approached by a beggar. Whether we are "caught" at stop lights, approached in parks, or have to pass "them" on the street, nothing so disturbs our tranquility as the thought of having to deal with a beggar. Just the anticipation of having to make eye contact with these particular individuals causes many people great anxiety. There may be many reasons for such distress: fear of violence, fear of being swindled, or, perhaps, disgust at what many consider to be laziness. All of these are possible reasons for the anxiety that stems from a possible confrontation with a beggar. It is a curious phenomenon, that a person poorly dressed, or barely dressed at all, asking for help is such a problem for Christians. That we are offered the opportunity to alleviate, even if only a small bit, the suffering of another human being strikes me as something Christians would joyously welcome. The reasons for why so many of us do fear or loathe beggars are beyond the scope of this book, but for many within the history of the church, almsgiving is not only an unequivocal good, but becoming one who begs can be a great good placed in the service of the church.[29]

Peter, who learned well from Francis, not only befriended beggars, but demanded that we see the role beggars play in Christianity. In his essay "Why Not Be a Beggar" he writes:

> People who are in need
>
> and are not afraid to beg
>
> give to people not in need
>
> the occasion to do good
>
> for goodness' sake.
>
> Modern society calls the beggar
>
> bum and panhandler
>
> and gives him the bum's rush.
>
> But the Greeks used to say
>
> that people in need
>
> are the ambassadors of the gods.
>
> Although you may be called
>
> bums and panhandlers
>
> you are in fact the Ambassadors of God.
>
> As God's Ambassadors
>
> you should be given food,
>
> clothing and shelter
>
> by those who are able to give it.[30]

The beggar is the Ambassador of God and, therefore, brings a bodily message to us in order to offer us an occasion to participate in the goodness of God. So it is not the giver who is the dominant charitable character

---

29. On the subject of begging, I know of no book better than Johnson's *The Fear of Beggars*.

30. Maurin, *Easy Essays*, 8.

in this story, rather it is the one who provides the other the occasion to practice such charity that occupies the position of prominence.

It would be a mistake, however, to assume that beggars primarily play the role of either a reminder of the need for justice, or the making of poverty a necessity. In her book *The Fear of Beggars*, Kelly Johnson reminds us that, ontologically, we are all beggars.[31] As we are mortal we not only petition other humans for the realization of our needs but we also plead to God for the care that God shows even the sparrows. For many of us, however, we are well aware that many sparrows, and humans, are better off than others. Some of us have houses while others have cardboard. Some of us have heat and air-conditioning while others suffer the torment of bitter winters and hot summers. Some of us have food while others go hungry. Though the Christian tradition allows us to have interesting conversations about what constitutes being better off it is good that all creatures have shelter, clothing, and food. Beggars remind us that such goods are never a given and as it is not a given, Christians maintain a special obligation to those that so heavily occupied the concern of both the prophets and Jesus. Johnson claims that beggars entertain a sacramental status as they are bodily reminders of the inequality that sustains our coveted way of life. These ambassadors of God, these that suffer and maintain better resources for understanding a crucified God than those who do not suffer, demand a faithful response. Beggars are sacramental because what they offer us is a

> . . . flash of an economy not based on fear and evasion of each other's needs, an economy that does not rely on rights as weaponry against the weakness of the human condition and against the need and demand of others. That flash is painful because the transition from the economy where a beggar is a parasite, morally deformed, or a metaphor for human mortality to an economy where this beggar could be a friend is shocking. They are a confrontation with the divine that most people can hardly bear to see and that they themselves may never know, if they are not recognized.[32]

Such recognition is difficult to achieve as much of the Christian protest that fuels our inability to give to the poor revolves around issues of merit, worth, or even fear. Many of us do not give to the homeless because we

---

31. Johnson, *The Fear of Beggars*, 197.

32. Ibid., 197–98.

"just know" they are going to spend their money on alcohol, or perhaps they are faking their need, or perhaps they are just indolent and prey on those respectable people like ourselves who, day in and day out, work hard for our money. Perhaps they mean to cause us and our families harm. Perhaps they just want to hurt us. Perhaps the ability to love without fear really is a gift from God (1 John 4:18).

In terms of dealing with issues of merit or worth, Chrysostom's assessment of those who would attempt to question and thus justify their denial of those who may or may not be in need is worth quoting:

> "But he fakes all that weakness and trembling," you tell me. And, saying so, you do not fear that a bolt of lightning will strike you from heaven? . . . You who fatten yourselves and enjoy your ease, you who drink well into the night, and then cover yourselves with soft blankets, . . . you dare demand a strict account from the needy who is little more than a corpse, and you fear not the account you will have to render before the court of Christ, terrible and frightful ? . . . We point out finger at the idleness of the poor, and yet we ourselves work at things that are worse than idleness . . . and you dare ask for an account.[33]

Chrysostom did not think it was the place of Christians to determine who was rightly in need. We spend so much of our time in pursuit of entertainment, careers, family, wealth, and a host of other things that Chyrsostom imagines being no better than idleness. Chrysostom warns us not to confuse being busy or in pursuit of lofty goals with being the opposite of laziness. Our fervent pursuits, even in our work, may be just as bad, or worse, than those that do nothing. Regardless, the central point is that inasmuch as we interrogate those who ask of our help God too will interrogate our lives, and this should be enough to keep the God-fearer away from such harsh judgments.[34]

The writer of Hebrews says, "Do not neglect to show hospitality to the stranger, for thereby some have entertained angels unawares" (13:2). The key word here is stranger. The stranger implies one that we know little to nothing about, for if we did what would be the achievement in helping one we know so well? That much should be a given. Jesus' demand that

33. Quoted in Howell's *Servants, Misfits, and Martyrs*, 110–11.

34. Chrysostom, *On Wealth and Poverty*, 53. This notion of certain forms of work being more problematic than not working at all is interesting and worthy of the kind of discussion I cannot offer in this book.

whatever we do for the "least of these" we do to him is enough to warrant careful attention to those who plead to us for help, without regard for our sake or the use of our money. It may be the case that there is no such thing as "our" money. Chrysostom tells us that our refusal to share our wealth with the poor deprives the poor of their very means for living. If so, it is necessary that we ask whether or not we can even continue to use words such as 'mine' or 'yours'.[35]

In her book *The Long Loneliness*, Day pauses to reflect on the following words by William James:

> We have grown literally afraid to be poor. We despise anyone who elects to be poor in order to simplify and save his inner life. If he does not join the general scramble, we deem him spiritless and lacking in ambition. We have lost the power even of imagining what the ancient realization of poverty could have meant; the liberation from material attachments, the unbribed soul, the manlier indifference, the paying our way by what we are and not by what we have, the right to fling away our life at any moment irresponsibly,—the more athletic trim, in short, the fighting shape.[36]

This continues to be the shape and posture of the Catholic Worker Movement. They live lives out of control, losing their life at any given moment so that they might gain it. They follow their leader who had neither a surplus of clothing nor a place to even lay his head, and in doing so are better able to welcome others like him. Their anarchistic brand of living should rightly be considered irresponsible by every good "responsible" *product* of this bureaucratic capitalist order. Their decrying of capitalism through their practices of charity and begging call into question whether or not there can even be a non-materialistic society under the banner of capitalism. Of course, their witness was no more determined by capitalism or materialism than any other privation of the good. Their way of life was determined only by their pursuit to be holy. They continually sought to live, at every moment, faithful to what they held to be true.

---

35. Ibid., 55.
36. Quoted in Day's, *The Long Loneliness*, 118–19.

4 *Clarence Jordan's Fellowship*

There is one thing you have got to learn about our movement.
Three people are better than no people.

—FANNIE LOU HAMER

One of things that the Catholic Worker thought was crucial to the construction of an order in which it was easier "for people to be good" was a return to the land. With the founding of agronomic universities, each person could participate in their own means of survival. Rather than functioning as passive consumers, people would grow their own food, build their own houses, and make their own clothes. Though this may sound idealistic or utopian, it is important to understand that the rationale for such a return stems from issues of justice. These Catholics were rightly attempting to best live out God's command to practice justice. Perhaps part of the answer resides in communal forms of living around the land? Even if it is but life shared together on a farm, such a practice has the potential to question what we too tacitly assume to be normative in terms of what it means to be human. As we will see in this chapter, many of our basic assumptions about what it means to be human, and what we think we may mean when we issue calls of freedom and justice, actually serve to endorse inherently racist ideologies. This is not necessarily a conscious endorsement, but is intrinsically dictated by the kind of politics necessary to sustain the nation-state. If so, it will demand that our Christian witness become anarchical in order that we can be liberated from the sinfulness of racism.

THE RACIST STATE (AND ITS DISCONTENTS)

*The notion that black people are human beings is a relatively
new discovery in the modern West.*

—CORNEL WEST

According to David Theo Goldberg, the development of the modern
nation-state depends upon racist categories for its emergence as a new
kind of politic.[1] Goldberg suggests that the development and ongoing
maintenance of the nation-state relies upon the instantiation of certain
racist norms for its intelligibility. Despite the Enlightenment's claims of
independence and equality, or, perhaps, because of these claims, embedded within the language of modernity are various conceptual and philosophical assumptions that make a kind of homogeneity of citizenship a
necessary prerequisite for political behavior. Essential to this homogeneity is one particular attribute: the color of one's skin.[2] Integral to the
discourse of modern politics are certain biological claims that supposedly inform us, from an objective scientific vantage-point, how best to
maintain the nation-state. Much of this objective vantage point assumes
various aesthetic, ethical, and biological norms as established by white
European thinkers.

Cornel West is another philosophical thinker that has illumined well
how the convergence of racism and modern thought are so intimately
tied. He argues that racism as a biological phenomenon is an inescapable
post-Enlightenment development as it was present in the very inception
of its language.[3] Though the development of modern biological racism

1. Goldberg, *The Racial State*.

2. In his *Race: A Theological Account*, J. Kameron Carter argues that it is within the
prevailing conditions established by much of theology's achievements within the West
that the biological account of racism is substantiated via various modern theological
movements. Carter does not simply suggest that biological racism was aided with the
help of theology as much as theology made possible the development of racism through
the natural sciences. Therefore, any response to the sinfulness of racism must occur
through theology.

3. Cornel West, *Prophesy Deliverance*, 47.

was contingent upon a number of factors that led to its rise, it may be the case that once certain factors are in play such racism becomes inevitable as certain norms are scripted into its discourse. The various forms of discourse, all of which assume a certain form of rationality, scientificity, and objectivity posit and assume a white norm by which everything else, including aesthetic categories, are judged.[4] This renders inevitable accounts of white supremacy that have narrated the past several centuries of Western civilization.

West argues that the language of freedom and equality cannot address the history of racism that modernity "secretes" because such "secretion" is the unavoidable result of the comparing and measuring of human bodies through the racist lens as established via the authority of Western science, Greek aesthetics, and Cartesian rationality.[5] These three categories underwrite western discourse and blinds western culture to its own inability to see how these are not objective discourses but already in fact privilege one culture, white European, over against others. In order to complete its task of making observations, science must assume some sort of ideal way of being, some normative gaze by which all things are judged. Though it remained hidden for centuries, West's genealogical deconstruction of this gaze exposes it as assuming certain classical forms of presentation, undergirded by a Cartesian dualism that privileges the mind over the body (the mind being the chief characteristic of what it means to be fully human) and rigid forms of scientific classification that categorizes humans as objects of study. That the white European would be viewed as the norm by which all other races would be evaluated leads to objective and scientific observations that those who are black, red, or yellow are simply, biologically speaking, less than human. It was for this reason that Immanuel Kant, perhaps *the* philosopher of modernity, at least in terms of establishing the parameters by which our speech and actions would be policed, claimed that the most vital organ of the human was the color of their skin.[6] The color of one's skin would tell you much

4. Ibid.

5. Ibid., 48.

6. See Kant, "Of the Different Human Races" in Bernasconi and Lott, *The Idea of Race*, 8–22. For a very enlightening reading of the profound effect the work of Kant had on establishing the biological and scientific case for racism see Bernasconi's "Who Invented the Concept of Race? Kant's Role in the Enlightenment Construction of Race." Bernasconi does not imagine that Kant is the sole author of the concept of race but that

about what you needed to know, scientifically, about a person's tempera-
ment, habits, abilities and personality. For example, in his lecture notes
of 1781/1782 Kant claimed that the "race of the Negroes, one could say,
is . . . full of affect and passion, very lively, chatty and vain. *It* can be
educated, but only to the education of servants, i.e., they can be trained.
They have many motives, are sensitive, fear blows and do much out of
concern for honor."[7] Throughout the majority of the twentieth century
there can be no mistaking that many, if not most, white Americans were
Kantian literalists.

The solution, however, does not simply rest in genealogical deconstruction. West does not imagine ignorance to be the root cause of
racism. Unfortunately, it is not simply a matter of "the more well-read
we are the less racist we will be." In fact, the very idea that racism is a
problem of ignorance privileges a culture that prizes education and intel-
ligence as a chief good amongst other goods. The notion that if one is
smart they will not be racist does nothing to combat how racism is built
in the very discourse that would suggest it could be overcome via a high-
priced education. Of course, racism and classism remain intertwined in
our culture, and the fact that some people in certain areas of our country
are not privy to the kind of education that could make them "less racist" remains a serious problem. The point for West, however, is that the
birth of modern biological racism occurs precisely alongside some of the
greatest philosophical and scientific achievements in the West and it cannot, therefore, be addressed within the very discourse that lends itself,
blindly, to racist assumptions. Racism is a part of the matrix of modernity
making our racist assumptions difficult to discern. We are conditioned to
imagine that this world is a world of our own making. It is an objectively
knowable world that can be free from bias if our thinking can only be
predicated on pure universal human reason. Yet it is this kind of modern
philosophical thinking that creates the kind of space in which we have
no choice but to assume certain norms for what constitutes the truly human. Those norms were inculcated and established by the very ones who
promised us a world where "we the people" could live as free and equal
partners in a new republic of our own making. Of course we can safely

---

if there is any one person who could be attributed with giving a theory of race "worthy of
the name" it would be Kant. (14)

7. Larrimore, "Sublime Waste: Kant and the Destiny of the Races" in Wilson,
Civilization and Oppression, 111–12. (Italics added.)

assume that "we the people" referred only to the white wealthy land and slave owners that drafted the Constitution. In this sense white racists like Matthew Hale, founder of the World Church of the Creator Movement, may be correct to suggest that their racist ideologies are more in line with the *original* authorial intent of the founders of the Constitution than those like Martin Luther King Jr. who read the Constitution as a promise of freedom for all humans. Racial minorities and women were simply not considered to be fully human, and hence equality and the pursuit of happiness was never intended for females or the non-white. Current white supremacist groups such as the Hammerskins or the Aryan Nation remind us that we should not be terribly surprised that a long standing racist order blossomed after the signing of the Constitution. Though the practices of racism was occurring prior to the drafting of this manuscript, what allowed it to blossom was the putting into print the very forms of life normative for the people of this newly conquered and colonized land. Though various forms of postmodern hermeneutics allow us the ability to read the Constitution in ways unimaginable by the writers of the Constitution, as if original authorial intent is always simple to determine or that attention to the historical context somehow determines the meaning of a text centuries later, it does suggest that what we cannot assume is the *meaning* of the words "freedom" and "equality."

Part of what has always driven the civil rights movement has been, and rightly so, the desire for each individual, regardless of the color of their skin, to be able to pursue a life of happiness on equal terms with any other person. West, however, is trying to show us that it is not this simple. It may be the case that part of the civil rights movement has only perpetuated this fundamentally racist order by seeking justice on the terms laid out by the very order being called into question. As D. Stephen Long argues in his book *The Goodness of God*, a society based on individual freedom and equality cannot recognize that *that* very language, freedom and equality, already privileges one culture over another. The language itself is one culture's imposition over others.[8] Such language stems from a hegemonic discourse that assumes certain characteristics as being normative for all yet, by its very self-assuming nature as the apex of human reason, is incapable of recognizing itself as being hegemonic.

8. D. Stephen Long, *The Goodness of God*, 200.

KING, X, AND A CIRCLED *A*

*An integrated cup of coffee is not sufficient pay
for four hundred years of slave labor.*

—MALCOLM X

A worthy case study of West and Long's criticism of the uncritical acceptance of the language of freedom and equality is found in Malcolm X's
hostility towards the civil rights movement. As is commonly known the
primary hero of the civil rights movement, Martin Luther King Jr., sought
the liberation of those deemed "colored" from their oppressors in hopes
that all people could live together peaceably in a just order. King sought
justice not just for the sake of the oppressed but also for the oppressor.
This was the radical call of Christian nonviolence that King demanded as
he correctly pointed out that whites needed to be saved from the tyranny
of their sin as much as black's needed to be saved from the tyranny of
whites. So for King, the purpose of the civil rights movement was not
simply a matter of inclusion into the white order, but a calling into account the basis of that very order.

Unfortunately, the primary language available to King was the language as found within the very culture that created racism. Though he
used the language of justice as promulgated through the prophets such as
Amos and Hosea, his understanding of freedom and equality was greatly
shaped by the order that was oppressing him. Malcolm X understood this
quite well. He understood that the problem with using the language of
civil rights is that it subordinates the issue of black oppression as being an
internal issue of the United States.[9] This creates an irresolvable antinomy
as once black suffering is construed as in internal political matter then it
can only be addressed in terms of the politics available within the United
States.[10] But if this is correct, that is, if the very liberalism upon which
the United States is predicated instantiates a doctrine of white supremacy

9. Instead of speaking of civil rights, Malcolm used the language of human rights.
I find this to be equally problematic, though for different reasons, as such language is
only available to Malcolm through one of the chief architects of the Enlightenment, John
Locke. Nevertheless, the point Malcolm was making was that the adoption of civil rights
locates the issue as one dictated by the confines of speech located only within the United
States.

10. D. Stephen Long, *The Goodness of God*, 200.

then the language of inclusivity and equality cannot work because such language assumes the normativity of white against which terms such as inclusivity and equality work.[11] These terms cannot be used without the assumption of such a norm and that is why they continue to fail to address the problem of racism.

What this meant for Malcolm X was the refusal to integrate with the very culture that created and demanded, philosophically, biologically and theologically, segregation. For Malcolm there was nothing morally or intellectually superior about such a culture. How could it be morally superior? It enslaved African-Americans for 400 years and Native-Americans for 500 years. Is it really an improvement to attain the level of equality that led whites to participate in such demonic practices? The answer for Malcolm was "no." For Malcolm there was nothing superior or even good about white culture so why would any moral human being wish to participate in it? Instead of integration, the only solution for Malcolm was a call for the privileging of African history and culture. This meant a total separation between whites and blacks. Blacks should form their own schools, their own businesses, their own economies, simply put, their own way of life.[12] It is important to note that Malcolm's claims for separation were made in light of the reality that blacks were *already* separate from whites. They were already separate but remained under the heavy hand of white oppression. Malcolm was only calling for freedom to control their own way of life. This is what differentiates separation from segregation. Segregation kept blacks under the control of whites making total separation the only chance of genuinely being freed from white exploitation. In terms of integration, he understood that if it were successful this would only make the black man an "honorary white man."[13] It simply makes the black person a person on terms laid about by white people. Malcolm could not see how this was much of an improvement. It leaves in tact the normativity of whiteness by which all others are gauged.

11. Ibid.

12. Ibid. D. Stephen Long points out that Malcolm X was not the first in American history to adopt this tactic. Roman Catholics, after discovering that the United States was a Protestant nation biased against the full inclusion of Catholics, founded their own schools and businesses.

13. Malcolm X astutely argued that the word "integration" was never clearly defined but was simply created as a means for avoiding what it was that 'blacks' wanted: respect as human beings. Malcolm X, *The Autobiography of Malcolm X*, 272.

Hence much of his invective leveled at King's desire for civil rights was Malcolm's calling King to accountability for risking becoming that which Malcolm considered to be, historically, nothing less than demonic.[14] Malcolm was concerned that King's call for civil rights did not really question the very thing that made such a call necessary. Malcolm was worried that whatever so-called advances King made, and for Malcolm if you imagine that gaining the right to use the same toilet as white people was progress then you were still a prisoner of the system, was only on the grounds paved by white people. For instance, in a televised debate with Gordon Hall, Hall referred to King as a "responsible American" which elicited this response from Malcolm: "When people like you usually refer to Negroes as responsible, you mean Negroes who are responsible in your context of *your type of thinking*."[15] Hall's comment proved to Malcolm the very point Malcolm was attempting to make about the poverty of white solutions and, hence, the lack of any real meaningful alternatives to the normativity of white culture. Malcolm's tactic, therefore, was altogether different from King's as Malcolm argued that the dominant culture of the United States was entirely bankrupt. Looking to it for inclusion or for answers, by using its language, only furthered the superiority assumed by white culture. Wanting in does not question the wickedness of this dominant culture; it merely presupposes the superiority of it.[16] Malcolm wanted to create a space for a different norm within the dominant culture (since a nation-wide trip back to Africa was, logistically, not possible) in which the standard of whiteness would not be assumed by seeking admittance in it, but by creating a culture that out-narrated it by its own way of life. Though there are many reasons for which Christians might disagree with Malcolm, this notion of separation, not necessarily of racial separation but of being a separate people should have at least, semantically, an appealing lure to the Christian.

14. Malcolm X's claim that the "white man is the devil" was an historical claim. The word "Satan" in Hebrew means "adversary" and Malcolm was correct to point out that, historically, there has never been any greater adversary to people 'of color' than the white people. Malcolm X, *The Autobiography of Malcolm X*, 266.

15. Breitman, *Malcolm X Speaks*, 182.

16. In King's defense, King was well aware of this and agreed with Malcolm that the last thing he wanted to do was become "co-exploiters" with his oppressors. King called not just for inclusion, but a completely different social order, one that was, much to the chagrin of many who champion King for their own benefit, based on socialism. See my article "Dethroning a King" where I argue that the subversive nature of King has been co-opted by the very orders he called into question.

The witness of both Malcolm and King is undeniably crucial for understanding issues of race and politics that continue to plague us today. In his analysis and comparison of the lives of both Malcolm X and Martin Luther King, James Cone suggests that it is better to understand how their arguments both complemented and corrected the other.[17] The levels of success they achieved were due to their ability to represent different sides of the same struggle to gain freedom—even if what they meant by freedom differed. The one thing they both agreed on was that blacks were owed respect as human beings, and Cone suggests that their different methods for gaining this respect enabled their success.

I think Cone is correct to suggest that King's life and testimony was a corrective to Malcolm's as much as Malcolm laid bare the ways in which inclusion often means assimilation and, thus, the destruction of black culture(s). The questions that arise between the corrective tensions of Malcolm X and Martin Luther King, Jr. are important for Christians in terms of how we address ongoing problems of both race and identity. It demands that we ask questions regarding our most determinative narratives. Malcolm once stated that he was not an American but was a victim of Americanism.[18] For Malcolm, his identity was rooted in a story other than the state. He found his story in the religion of Islam. For Christians this requires that we ask certain questions about which narrative is our primary narrative, and how we answer those questions determines how we address issues of race. We locate the kind of witness required in order to reveal not simply the problem of racism but the sin of racism. But if these thinkers are correct in their arguments about the poverty of liberalism then what sort of language must be employed to address the sin of racism? And if King's vision of a more just earth in which all people live harmonious is an engaging vision then what language and forms of life must be practiced in order that we do not fall prey to Malcolm's concern that we simply end up perpetuating an order that refuses real change by assimilating those that would change it?

I imagine it is beyond any one person to be able to answer well these questions. If so, this would undo part of the necessity of Christian accountability. I began this chapter with a quote from the great civil rights activist Fannie Lou Hamer. One of the aspects about her life that I find so

---

17. Cone, *Martin and Malcolm and America*, 288–318.

18. Breitman, *Malcolm X Speaks*, 26.

appealing is that while being imprisoned or being pressed for answers to racial problems she would often begin to, quite loudly, sing hymns. I think there may be more significance to such an approach than most are willing to grant. Regardless, whenever I think of her comment that three people are better than no people, the third person I think of (and I beg forgiveness for taking her quote out of context) is Clarence Jordan. Without in any way dismissing the truthfulness of the witness of both Malcolm X and King, I will examine another path, the path of Clarence Jordan. Much of Jordan's activities was shaped prior to the civil rights movement but also peaked at the height of the movement. I do not think his path is by any means at odds with King's path, as King spoke fondly of Jordan, rather I find it to be complementary to both the concerns that weighed so heavily on both King and Malcolm X. And this is definitely not an attempt to suggest that a white man has answers to black problems. I would be rightly called out for even hinting at such a suggestion. On issues of race white people need to first practice silence and listening before offering words of help as otherwise we fall prey to Malcolm's worry that a white solution to a black problem is not a solution for blacks but for whites.[19] However, racism is not just a problem, it is a sin. Therefore as Christians, we who are baptized out of our whiteness, must attempt to embody our baptisms in a way that reveals racism as sinful and at odds with God's peaceable kingdom. I merely look toward Jordan because he tried to embody an alternative way of life that was not dependent upon the state, or its discourse, for its intelligibility. In this sense, I envision the life of Jordan as a complementary path to that of King's and Malcolm X's.

THE COTTON-PATCH MAN

It is not enough to limit your love to your own nation, to your own group. You must respond with love even to those outside of it. . . . This concept enables people to live together not as nations, but as the human race.

—CLARENCE JORDAN

Favorably known as the "theologian in overalls," Clarence Jordan was a person of hard work and sharp wit. Once when he was being paraded

---

19. On the issue of the social context from which our non-objective theology arises, and what this means for white participation in black speech on God, race, and issues pertaining to justice see James Cone's *God of the Oppressed*, 1–35.

through the inside of a rather opulent church the minister of the church took Jordan outside to watch the sun set over the steeple. As the earth's rotations placed itself in just the right place, the sun cast a beautiful spotlight on the majestic cross that crowned the top of the church. The minister boasted to Jordan, "That cross alone costs us ten thousand dollars." Jordan looked at the cross and then looked back at the minister and matter-of-factly stated, "You got cheated. Times were when Christians could get them for free."[20] Jordan always knew how to get straight to the point.

Clarence Jordan was born on July 29, 1912 in the small town of Talbotton, Georgia. One of seven children, his father was a prosperous banker capable of providing well for his family. Jordan grew up in a comfortable home that was also ripe with strong Baptist convictions. Like all other children growing up in the South, or anywhere else in the United States for that matter, he was raised in the center of a racially divided environment. This was, to say the least, a complex environment. Centuries of racism remains entrenched within the history of the United States. In his book *The Hidden Wound*, the southern poet and farmer Wendell Berry attempts to come to terms with what he claims to be the fated crisis of racial awareness:

> [T]he sense of being doomed by my history to be, if not always a racist, then a man always limited by the inheritance of racism, condemned to be always conscious of the necessity *not* to be a racist, to be always dealing deliberately with the reflexes of racism that are embedded in my mind as deeply at least as the language I speak.[21]

Due to our own history we are fated to contend with this prejudice that infiltrates our actions and our language—even the unspoken. Berry describes the racial silence he grew up with in the South that was some three to four hundred years in the making prior to his birth. This silence stood between him and one of his immediate heroes, Nick, a black farm worker on the Berry farm. The young Wendell was, at the time, unaware of the severity and depth of the wound. It was in the 1940's and Berry was just a child. Berry's first awareness of this silent wound came when his family gave him a birthday party and he was allowed to invite whomever he

---

20. Wallis and Hollyday, *Cloud of Witnesses*, 60.
21. Berry, *The Hidden Wound*, 49.

wished. Unaware of the social manners of the day he invited Nick. Nick, of course, knew well the social awkwardness the young boy had created, yet felt obliged to attend. Nick came to the party, but he did not enter the house. He remained outside and sat on the cellar wall. Becoming aware of the rules that had been broken by the invitation an older Berry reflects, "I had done a thing more powerful at the time; I had scratched the wound of racism, and all of us, our heads beclouded in the social dream that all was well, were feeling the pain."[22]

As another white southerner, Jordan too became aware of the unspoken in a haunting way. Despite his own protestant tradition's complicity with racist policies, ideologies, and practices, it was his ecclesial formation that first broke this racial silence. Though there were members of his own Baptist church who would sing hymns one moment and were found torturing blacks the next, Jordan, also at a young age, understood the egalitarian claims of a familiar children's hymn:

> Jesus loves the little children,
>
> All the children of the world;
>
> Red and yellow, black and white,
>
> They are precious in His sight;
>
> Jesus loves the little children of the world.[23]

Though he was young, Jordan understood the vast gap between the singing of this song and the ability of his neighbors to understand its implications. Due to the unsettling awareness of how his white Christian brothers and sisters lived lives incongruent with what they sang he decided that something more direct was needed in order to overcome the oppressive conditions forced onto blacks. When he graduated from high school he decided to study agriculture as a means of embodying the profound meaning of this children's song. Jordan imagined that it would be through the local farm that racism, and the forced poverty created by racism, would be overcome.

The Depression, however, took its toll on the Jordan family. The family lost much of its money and Jordan was no longer sure that his embrace of scientific farming (the development of more efficient means of tilling the land) would satisfy all of life's needs. After college he en-

22. Ibid., 53.

23. This is recounted in McClendon's *Biography as Theology*, 91.

tered Southern Baptist Theological Seminary in Louisville, Kentucky in the hopes of discovering answers to the problems caused not only by the Depression, but the violence that flows from racism. In order to accomplish this task, Jordan graduated with a Ph.D. in Greek New Testament from Southern Baptist Theological Seminary. This is not exactly the kind of degree one thinks of in terms of addressing issues of social justice. Yet, if there was going to be an answer to how to approach these problems of poverty, violence, and racism, then Jordan imagined it had to be found in the New Testament. He was determined, therefore, to be able to read it as accurately as possible. For Jordan, this meant reading it in Greek.

Of course, one need not have to read the New Testament in Greek in order to read it well, but what it did require of Jordan was an intimate knowledge with the sayings of and about Jesus. In reference to the systemic evils that Jordan found plaguing his time, there were several passages he considered crucial for Christian thought and practice: Acts 2:44, Gal 3:28, and Matt 5:1–7:27. The latter passage is the Sermon on the Mount and it was this text, along with the entire story of Jesus and the prophetic calling of the suffering servant in the Old Testament, which convinced Jordan that discipleship required a life of nonviolence as well as a radical spirit of forgiveness. If the Son of God could be innocently executed by the very powers that he came to redeem and would, nevertheless, redeem creation through forgiveness, then it is must be assumed that Christians must also enact this radical form of forgiveness. For Jordan, Christian witness entails more than the preaching of a crucified God; one must be willing to enact the story of this crucified God. Nonviolence, love of the enemy, and the forgiveness of one's persecutor, even when they are not seeking it, were "givens" for Jordan. His reading of the Sermon on the Mount demanded an acceptance of nonviolence. It was while he was in ROTC, which he had previously not found to be problematic, that he started to sense a conflict between Jesus' demand to love one's enemies and the learning of how to strategically fire bullets into other human beings. During a target practice session he came to the conclusion that there was no way to reconcile following Jesus with armed service. After he unloaded most of his bullets into dummies he said, "I was shaking as if I were having chills. And it was crystal clear that this Jesus was going one way or another. Yet I called myself his follower."[24] Jordan, after explaining

---

24. Snider, The "Cotton Patch" Gospel: The Proclamation of Clarence Jordan, 10.

to his commanding officer that he could not simultaneously serve the God of Jesus and the god of war, refused his commission and entered directly into seminary.

The other two passages, Gal 3:28 and Acts 2:44, provided specifics as to how to address the twin problems of racism and involuntary poverty. For Jordan, these issues were conflated as it was the case that blacks were amongst the poorest of the poor. As both King and Malcolm X argued, this was no accident—it was by design. It was the brutality of the principalities and powers that created and maintained a network of relations that systematically oppressed black people. It was these principalities and powers that had to be named and resisted if one was going to consider themselves a Christian. The problem, however, rested in the fact that it was not simply the state that was the sole oppressor, it was the white church buttressing the victimization created by the state. It was, for Jordan, the white southern church that had shackled the ankles and wrists of blacks and, in doing so, had shackled Jesus and made him a slave to their own twisted understanding of the good. Jordan, finding no small amount of theological ammunition to use against this apostate church, persistently preached Gal 3:27–29:

> As many of you as were baptized in Christ and have clothed yourselves in Christ. There is no longer Jew or Greek, there is no longer slave or free, there is no longer male or female; for all of you are one in Jesus Christ. And if you belong to Christ, then you are Abraham's offspring, heirs according to the promise.

His own translation of Gal 3:27–28 reads as follows:

> You who were initiated into the Christian fellowship are Christian allies. No more is one white and another a Negro; no more is one a slave and the other a free man; no longer is one male and the other a female. For you all are as one in Christ Jesus. And if you are Christ's men, then you are the true "white men," noble heirs of a spiritual heritage.[25]

---

25. Jordan, *The Cotton Patch Version of Paul's Epistles*, 99. Jordan's cotton patch translations of the Bible are not intended to be historically accurate translations, but translations that place scripture in the specific context of the reader with the intention of helping the reader understand scriptural implications. His translation of Galatians is written as "The Letter to the Churches of the Georgia Convention."

By translating Paul's letter to the Galatians as letters to the white southern churches of Georgia, Jordan was attempting to reveal the fundamentally dissident nature of Jesus' life. Jesus' disciples should not support a political order predicated on the subordination of some humans to others; rather, Jesus' disciples should be calling it into question by their very form of life. Once one is baptized there is no longer male nor female, Jew nor Greek, black nor white (nor red nor yellow), there is only one body: the body of Christ. Jordan demanded that Christians acknowledge and live into this one body. This does not eradicate all differences, as if, biologically speaking women or men no longer exist; rather, it calls into question the kind of relationships that are constitutive of these differences by placing these differences under the inclusive and ontologically-constituting banner of baptism. The body of the Christian is now narrated by the claims made on it by Christ as opposed to the numerous ideologies placed on it in this time between times. If Christians are to live non-secular lives then we must live into our baptisms. Though living into our baptisms may look like a variety of things, they must somehow reveal how it is that we are no longer Jew nor Greek, black nor white. For an answer to the shape this may take, Jordan offered an experiment in Christian living that continues to provide us with a glimpse of God's peaceable kingdom.

THE DEMONSTRATION PLOT

Faith is not belief in spite of evidence but a life lived in scorn of the consequences.

—CLARENCE JORDAN

In 1942 Jordan and his wife Florence, along with another couple, Martin and Mabel England, moved to a 440 acre plot of land near Americus, Georgia to create an interracial Christian farming community.[26] Despite the land being completely barren, save one seedling pecan tree, Jordan referred to it as a demonstration plot for the Kingdom of God. It would be on this desolate plot of land that the Jordans would attempt to embody

---

26. The Englands had already experimented with communal living in Wakefield, Kentucky and desired to attempt to break down racial divides in the United States by creating an interracial farming commune. It was Jordan's meeting with Martin England that inspired Jordan's eventual leadership of *Koinonia*.

the call of Christian living. They called it "The *Koinonia* Farm." The basis of *Koinonia*, which means "fellowship" or "communion," stems from Acts 2:44–47:

> All who believed were together and had all things in common; they would sell their possessions and goods and distribute the proceeds to all, as any had need. Day by day, as they spent much time together in the temple, they broke bread at home and ate their food with glad and generous hearts, praising God and having the good will of all people. And day by day the Lord added to their number those who were being saved.

Jordan surmised that if this sort of communal living was the standard practice in the early church, then why not now? Had this call to live in community, to share goods or to sell one's own possessions to provide for others expired? How should Christians respond to this passage, and did it have anything to say to the non-racist character of God's Kingdom?

Jordan wanted to give a simple answer to what he thought was a difficult question. A return to the practices of the early church, as well the example of various monastic and Anabaptist intentional communities, was necessary if Christians were going to be able to better understand the nature of their call to be in but not of this world. Jordan created four simple premises that would underwrite their common life: 1) Treat all people with dignity, 2) refuse to respond to violence with violence, 3) the sharing of all possessions, and 4) the practice of careful stewardship of the land loaned to us by God. By practicing these four tenets, Jordan hoped to not only be faithful to the witness of the New Testament, but to expose how accommodating the American Christian had become towards the world. This was to be a community providing a prophetic witness against the structures of militarism, materialism, and racism. This was not, however, its first task. Its first task was to take Jesus at his word when he, time and time again, told those that would follow him and wish to be perfect to give what possessions they had to the poor. As Charles Marsh claims, *Koinonia* was constructed on the hermeneutical decision to practice the way of Jesus in their daily lives and work. Its primary goal was not to be the center of the civil rights movement but to experiment with the path of Christ.[27] This meant the refusal to show either favoritism

---

27. Marsh, *The Beloved Community*, 67–69.

or prejudice against anyone. All of life would be integrated toward one goal, the worship of God.

Part of the scandal of the *Koinonia* Farm was that it asked its members to become completely dispossessed. By dispossessed I do not mean only in the sense of objects—though this is undoubtedly part of it. If this was going to be a demonstration plot for the Kingdom of God then participants would have to die to their self. Full-fledged members (the farm hosted many people from various Christian denominations who were not required to give up everything) held no private possessions as every basic necessity was covered by a common purse. This practice alone was enough to warrant suspicion from those who suspected *Koinonia* to be a communist front. This was a true sign, thought Jordan, that such critics possessed little knowledge of either Christianity or communism.[28] Nevertheless, the idea that people would give up what they rightfully earned was simply an affront to the well-schooled ears of most American Christians. Anyone who gave up their possessions to share and live communally with others was, naturally, assumed to be seditious.

What made matters worse was that the *Koinonians* accepted black people into their experiment. If this were to be a true demonstration plot of God's kingdom then no one could be excluded. Jordan, along with some of the other *Koinonians*, had already been excommunicated from their local Baptist churches for bringing black people to church. To make matters worse, they were now issuing invitations to live with people of other races. Though it is true that the majority of participants who became fully fledged members of *Koinonia* were white, the fact that blacks worked on this farm, lived on this farm, worshipped on this farm, and broke bread on this farm was just too much for the Sumter County residents to handle. This experiment had to be put to a stop and it would be the local God-fearing Christian residents who would do it.

After more than a decade of fairly peaceful existence, the neighbors of *Koinonia* had enough. By 1956 matters were such that residents of *Koinonia* regularly had to dodge not only bullets but explosives intent on killing these "race-mixers." There was constant vandalism and damage done to the farm. Each person suffered persistent death threats and even their children were not spared from the harsh invective of their own school teachers who chided them in front of their classmates for being communists.

28. Lee, *Cotton Patch Evidence*, 131.

Though the death threats and bullets were damaging enough to the community, what almost resulted in their demise was the economic boycott leveled against the farm. Jordan could no longer buy seeds for crops, or purchase gasoline for their tractors. They could no longer procure insurance for their houses, farms, or farming equipment. Banks refused to do business with them and because no one would buy, sell or trade with them, they faced near collapse.

Since growing crops was next to impossible, they were able to manage marketing pecans. During the next several years, they began shelling pecans and finding buyers, primarily from out of state, who were willing to buy from them. With typical Jordan wit their slogan was, "Shipping the Nuts Out of Georgia." This kept *Koinonia* afloat while the threats, shootings, and boycott slowly, throughout the early 1960s, ceased.

Despite finding a new means of survival, the constant persecution of the farm took its toll. By 1963 only four adults remained living on the farm. Though many would continue to volunteer their time to this attempt to embody Jordan's vision of Christian practice, it was clear that something would have to change or the farm would perish. Today, *Koinonia* still sells Pecans, but it is primarily famous for being the birthplace of Habitat for Humanity. In 1968, Millard and Linda Fuller visited *Koinonia* and decided that what was needed was better housing for the poor of Georgia. One year after this change in direction, just prior to the first house being built, Clarence Jordan died of a heart attack. Yet his vision for peace, racial reconciliation, and justice towards the poor and oppressed live on in not only Americus but throughout the world due to its association with Habit for Humanity International and The Fuller Center for Housing.

PROTESTING PROTEST

[T]he "truth" of . . . revolt against the Establishment is the emergence of a new establishment in which transgression is part of the game . . .

—SLAVOJ ŽIŽEK

Though there is much to learn from the on-going witness of *Koinonia*, what may be most important is the manner in which they approached issues of race, economics, and violence. They did not offer theories, or dissertations as solutions, nor did they demand that the government or state officials create the solution. To be sure, Jordan did write and speak often about such issues and his Cotton-Patch translations were intent on changing how Christians viewed one another. Jordan, however, imagined that the best way to combat racism, violence, and poverty was to live in such a way that one's life became an alternative to these injustices. Jordan never marched against Washington nor did he ever ask his senators to do what he felt he was personally called to do. He did not imagine these to be bad things; these were just not the ways he thought he could most affect change. On a recent documentary about *Koinonia* his daughter even tells of her father's reluctance to support her as she marched, illegally, down the city streets demanding equal rights for African Americans.[29] It is not that Jordan thought that she should not stand up to unjust laws, he simply thought that the most direct action one could take was to first and foremost live the change sought.

This remains a rather contested point of debate for those that reflect thoroughly on Jordan's life. On one hand, Jordan is, indirectly or not, calling into question the primary approach King and other civil right's leaders employed in order to enact the change rightfully desired by millions within America. In his book *The Beloved Community*, Charles Marsh briefly discusses this when he claims that Jordan's experimental plot is best remembered as "an exercise in repentance, reconciliation, and costly discipleship—not as a solution to the race problem."[30] In one sense, Marsh is correct. The civil rights movement was successful at ending segregation, gaining the vote, and bettering conditions altogether for blacks. This was something well outside the reach of *Koinonia*. However, to say that it is not a solution to the race problem seems to miss the point. Marsh rightly speaks of *Koinonia* as a community of disciples seeking reconciliation and repentance. They do so because they understand racism is not just a problem, it is a sin. Jordan imagined that by participating in this integrated community of disciples they could show the world the kind of God they serve. Such a glimpse would, hopefully, serve as a corrective to the powers that exploited human beings.

It is true that in this regard, much of this nation has yet to participate in this experience of repentance, reconciliation, and discipleship. To that

29. See the documentary "Briars in the Cotton Patch: The Story of Koinonia Farm," Cotton Patch Productions, 2003.

30. Marsh, *The Beloved Community*, 84.

point I will return at the end of the book. For now, however, I think it is vital to recognize the kind of anarchism that fueled the witness of Jordan. It was not the kind that ever courted trouble, even for noble reasons, but anticipated that enough trouble would court them if they participated in the kind of life they thought best reflected the peaceable kingdom. Jesus never sought to break the law, and there is much in scripture, as we will see in the next chapter, that demands that Christians practice subordination to even unjust laws. At the same time, Jesus practiced an almost holy indifference to the law as he never sought to break them but refused to live accordingly to those laws that were at odds with his kingdom. Though he never pursued trouble per se, he was, nevertheless, accused of being a rabble rouser and was executed according to Roman law. Jesus was executed not because he attempted to change the way Romans constructed their laws, nor for attempting to gain office and legislate his beliefs. He was executed because he gathered a people that posed a viable threat to the stability of worldly powers. Jesus threatened the status quo by creating an alternative community that called into question various branches of Judaic traditions as well as Roman customs. By gathering a people who live differently than the world, Jesus and his followers call into question the legitimacy of the so-called norm. This is at the heart of what Jordan was attempting to do. It is not that he thought protesting an unjust law was wrong, but, and this is my argument, perhaps he thought it too easy. This is not to suggest that protest is not courageous, for it often represents the epitome of bravery. The act of protest has cost many their lives and families, so it should be faithfully remembered. At the same time, a certain kind of protest has become but another trend within this culture that, ironically, buttresses the very thing being called into question. Protest is now scripted. It is part of the fabric of democracy that its leaders continually tell us "makes us so great" in comparison to the rest of the nations. This very well may be true. But it is also the case that protesting and lobbying for governments to create conditions that will still be ruled by those governing bodies is a pale comparison to those capable of creating an alternative to the very thing that is the ire and cause of one's protest. Semantically the word "protest" suggests being "for" something, not against. The creation of alternative manners of living, whether it is in the form of alternative economies or alternative relationships, requires far more work than carrying signs and gathering around municipal buildings. Again, this should not be read as a claim that the witness of

Jordan is either antithetical to or more faithful than that of King's legacy. I am also not suggesting that marching is bad or lacks courage. The contrarian in me enjoys a good protest as my fascination with the two priests in the following chapter proves. In terms of the witness of both King and Jordan, I think there is much overlap in their strategies. Christian witness is never monolithic and it requires a wide variety of approaches and experimentation. This is a good thing and should be celebrated. It is just that for Jordan his calling was to create an alternative community whose very presence in the world offers the world an alternative to its' self. He did not demand a different kind of government; rather, he participated in a movement that attempted to be that which we may hopefully call both good and just. In this manner, Jordan lived life both apocalyptically and eschatologically. He attempted to embody the very notion that the kingdom of God is here right now, and so he lived life as if it were to be a witness to life prior to the fall of creation—as well as after the final redemption of creation. He offered an eschatological witness to the way the world was created, was meant to be and will one day be. He offered food, friendship, love, and most of all, hope. In this manner, I think the dual witness of King and Jordan, the insight of Malcolm X, as well as the countless witnesses against racism that include people such as Sojourner Truth and Fannie Lou Hamer, offers us the kind of resources by which we can faithfully reside in, but not of, Babylon.

5 *The Brothers Berrigan*

And they shall beat their swords into plowshares, and their spears into pruning hooks; nation shall not lift up sword against nation; neither shall they learn war anymore.

—ISAIAH 2:4

Isaiah, we are told, fell a martyr to the same powers who had earlier sought his counsel; swords into plowshares became a hot political item, not to be tolerated by the warrior state.

—DANIEL BERRIGAN

On September 9, 1980, two Catholic priests named Daniel and Philip Berrigan, along with six other activists, entered a General Electric nuclear weapons plant in Pennsylvania armed with hammers and vials of their own blood. The eight activists beat on multiple unarmed nuclear nosecones as a symbolic yet literal protest against Christian complicity in the construction of nuclear missiles. After hammering away on the nosecones, vividly calling forth images of Isa 2:4, Mic 4:3 and Joel 3:10, the activists poured their own blood on these weapons and concluded their protest by offering prayers for peace and justice. The aforementioned prophets claim that after the coming of the Messiah God's people will beat their weapons into plowshares and cease the learning of war. According to these Christians, the Messiah has come and they want the world to know it. Thus, the Plowshares Movement was born. Though they were all arrested and charged with more than ten different felony and misdemeanor counts, their actions would be repeated multiple times with each one earning the priests, and their fellow activists, significant time in prison.

While Clarence Jordan shied away from illegal protests, the Berrigan brothers thrived on it. Though it cost them many years in jail, these two

Christian anarchists broke countless laws they felt were contrary to God's intentions for the world. I imagine it remains rather scandalous to the Catholic Church that two of her most well known priests, Daniel and Philip Berrigan, share something in common with the notorious Al-Qaeda leader Osama Bin Laden: all three have been on the Federal Bureau of Investigation's Top Ten Most Wanted List. Though I doubt the Berrigans, or Bin Laden for that matter, would appreciate such a comparison, it is important to remember that the FBI only places on its list those they deem a serious threat to the well-being of its republic. That a couple of Midwestern Catholic priests have shared the bill with one of the most well known terrorists of the twentieth and twenty-first centuries is surely more than an interesting bit of trivia. What could possibly inspire the FBI to place these brothers on a list that includes rapists, terrorists, drug traffickers, and serial killers? Surely the ongoing destruction of government property might warrant this, along with the decision by the Berrigans to go, for a time, underground in order to elude authorities. I wonder, however, if it has a more intimate connection with the reasons that led an earlier empire to execute a poor Jew from Galilee for demanding love of enemies and economic redistribution? Jesus' upside kingdom was too threatening for the powers that be so he had to be killed. That his followers would end up being enemies of the same powers that killed their leader should not be surprising; perhaps it should even be expected. But as Augustine correctly stated it is not the punishment that makes one a martyr, it is the cause.[1] What is important for us is to examine the cause that drove the Berrigans to be at such divisive odds with the practices of the American Empire.

I FOUGHT THE LAW AND THE LAW . . . ?

God may tell us not to kill, but when the state calls we must obey.

—PHILIP BERRIGAN

Daniel Berrigan (May 9, 1921) and his brother Philip (October 5, 1923–December 6, 2002) were born, respectively, in Virginia and Two Harbors, Minnesota. Their family, including their mother, father and four other brothers, were hardworking middle class Irish Catholics. Though their

---

1. Paolucci, *The Political Writings of St. Augustine*, 185.

father eventually left the Catholic Church, both Daniel and Philip became her ambassadors. Daniel joined the Jesuits after graduating from high school while Philip joined a Josephite Seminary. Philip's entry into the priesthood came much later than Daniel's. After attending college for less than a year, Philip was drafted into the military in order to serve in World War II. It was during his time in the military that Philip became highly conscious of not only his eventual protest and revulsion of killing, but of militant racism. For Philip, much of the manner in which soldiers were taught how to demonize their enemies, making it possible for them to kill them, was already being learned by white Americans against black Americans. While sailing for Scotland, Philip came to the conclusion that the United States, in 1943, was, despite the emancipation of blacks some seventy-five years earlier, still two separate and entirely unequal nations. The white troops slept in warm staterooms filled with beds and blankets while the black troops slept on the decks, huddled together and suffering from exposure to the brutal elements of rain and ice.[2] Philip's concern, as with Jordan's, King's and the Catholic Worker, for how protests against violence incorporated all aspects of life remained prominent fixtures in his life.

By the mid-1960s the Berrigans became adamant protestors of the Vietnam War. It was not just their stance on violence, but their ability to see how racism, militarism, and materialism were so thoroughly intertwined in this war. They understood well how the Vietnam War was about posturing, economic gain, and the poor whites and blacks who would die for it. The Berrigans could not consider themselves faithful practitioners of the gospel if they were not courageous enough to take a committed stand against the war. So they preached, wrote articles and letters to their representatives, and Philip even protested at the home of the Secretary of Defense in Washington, DC. This latter move, unappreciated by both state and church authorities, landed him a transfer to Baltimore, Maryland.

Though Philip understood his transfer as a serious reprimand by the church he refused to be silent. On October 17, 1967, along with the Rev. James Mengel, David Eberhardt and Tom Lewis, Philip walked into a Baltimore Customs House and poured their own blood on Selective

---

2. Berrigan, *Fighting the Lamb's War*, 16.

Service Records.[3] This group, known as the Baltimore Four, decided that in an effort to protest the blood being spilt in Vietnam they would spill their own blood. The action of using blood has other symbolic reasons as well given that it is such an important motif throughout the Bible. Blood represents life. The spilling of it in the Bible, even from nonhuman animals, is a serious event. That Jesus' blood was spilled so that blood sacrifice was no longer necessary is an important part of Christian theology. The Baltimore Four was well aware of this theological point. The shedding of their blood, which resulted in a prison sentence, was a symbolic act that was designed to shock the sleeping masses into awareness of the wickedness of the Vietnam War. By using blood, the group hoped that a nation with at least a passing familiarity with scripture would better understanding the extremity of their actions. For the most part, it did not.

After being released on bail, Philip enlisted the help of a slightly larger group of activists, later dubbed the Catonsville Nine. This time, after long prayerful consideration, his brother Daniel participated. They walked into the draft board of Catonsville, Maryland, poured blood on almost four hundred draft files and then torched them with the use of homemade napalm. The reason for using napalm was also symbolic as it was being dropped on the Vietnamese. The horror of napalm is that it clings to the surface of whatever it is burning. The "stop, drop and roll" technique does not deter the flames. It remains on a person's skin, slowly burning them. That the nine of them prayerfully awaited their arrest and spent several years in prison for their action speaks volumes as to what the government holds dear: medals for those who burn humans, prison for those who burn paper.

Their time in prison, however, neither deterred nor "rehabilitated" them. Prison only fueled their cause. The Berrigans understood their time behind bars as the logical consequence of following the one who promised that his disciples would be hated and persecuted. That Jesus was killed as according to the dictates of law was a hermeneutic employed by the Plowshares Eight as a reference for better understanding who writes and enacts the law. In an era of legalized racism, legalized poverty, and lawful weapons capable of mass destruction of millions, what else can a Christian do but put their body between those who are innocent and

---

3. Mengel donated his blood but did not pour it. He passed out literature to the draft-board workers as well the police officers who responded to the scene.

those who would harm the innocent? It was especially their fight against the development of nuclear bombs that garnered their strongest resistance as nuclear weapons make everything else a moot point:

> The fact that we are complicit in the presence of bomb—because we help pay for it, we allow its deployment and possible use . . . destroys us spiritually, morally, psychologically, emotionally, and humanly. Our complicity in the bomb makes us incapable of dealing with lesser social and political problems that are in reality spin-offs of our dedication to the bomb.[4]

Much of what fueled the Berrigan protest against the militarism of the United States was their understanding that the manufacturing of nuclear missiles could result in the destruction of everything. Nothing goes unscathed in the construction of nuclear missiles. Even if they are never used, the trillions of dollars spent on them murders the poor. Money that could have been allocated for the well-being of the poor is put into service for the possible destruction of all things. There is nothing but madness that causes us to permit the making of nuclear weapons. Just prior to the death of Philip in 2002, he stated that he would "die with the conviction, held since 1968 and Catonsville, that nuclear weapons are the scourge of the earth, that to mine them, manufacture them, deploy them, and use them is a curse against God, the human family, and the earth itself."[5]

Due to their protest against war the Berrigans became quite accustomed to the inside of federal courtrooms. In their defense they would often employ what is known as the Necessity Defense. An example of the Necessity Defense goes as follows: If a room full of children were on fire it would be permissible, according to the law, to damage the door by breaking it down in order to save the children. In such a case as this no court of law would justly hold accountable the one who broke down the door to save the children. In terms of attempting to halt the construction of nuclear weapons, weapons that cannot discriminate between combatants and non-combatants the Berrigans claimed this defense in light of the International Tribunal's judgment at Nuremberg which states that individuals have international duties which transcend the national obligations of obedience imposed by the individual state. According to this international law, if a citizen has knowledge of an action by their own

4. Dear, *You Will Be My Witnesses*, 154–55.
5. Ibid., 156.

state that can cause undue harm to others, then that citizen has an obligation to the international community that supersedes their particular
national community. No more would there be instances of people claiming, as did German officers and soldiers during WWII, that they were just
doing what they were told. Each individual citizen is responsible to more
than just their national identity. With this line of defense, the Berrigans
reasoned that since they have full knowledge of what will happen via the
use of nuclear weapons on other countries then they have a "responsibility to prevent these crimes."[6] Their appeals to International Law, when
even recognized by the state's judges, were not persuasive.

The Berrigan's brand of confrontational actions revolved around the
manner in which so much of American life, that which many of us call
"blessings from God," is made possible by an unbridled militarism hardly
rivaled in history. Whether it is issues of national security or matters of
economic dependency on two-third's world resources, our way of life is
sustained by the more than seven hundred American military bases spread
throughout the world. The direct actions of the Berrigans stemmed from
their desire to awaken the American people to their complicity in a war-
making machine. Christians are called to be peacemakers. We are called
to love our enemies, to turn our cheeks, and to pray for our persecutors.
This is the opposite of pre-emptive strikes, nuclear preparedness, and
even self-defense. Their understanding of Jesus does not allow any room
for violence perpetrated onto others. This renders them treasonous to
the popular brand of Christianity in North America. Christ, the market,
law and violence go so well together in the United States. To question the
connections is to apostatize from the empire's religion.

AMERICAN CIVIL RELIGION & ROMANS 13

In God we trust, because He's one of us.

—BAD RELIGION (*AMERICAN JESUS*)

For many Christians in the United States the Berrigans are a tough pill to
swallow. Their prophetic challenge to the state bothers many of us because
it challenges us to see how we are complicit in its machinations. It is not
that the Berrigans, as some claim, are anti-patriotic (they are not, they

---

6. Berrigan, *Fighting the Lamb's War*, 187.

are simply anti-idolatry), it is that what constitutes the majority of people working to keep this republic going are, at least nominally, Christians. It has been assumed for some time that to be a good American (and I use that term loosely as I am only referring to the United States of America) is to be a good Christian. One of the primary myths of this nation-state is that it is a chosen nation. Ranging from American history textbooks to evangelists on television, many of this nation's commentators are convinced that, sans the natives here prior to our arrival, this land's inhabitants are the chosen people of God. This is known as the myth of American exceptionalism.[7] It is the idea that the citizens of the United States are the chosen people of God destined with a special mission and purpose to reveal to the world. What once belonged to the nation of Israel and the church is now subsumed by the American people. Jews and Christians can be a part of God's chosen people but only through our participation in the maintenance of the empire. Of course what this often means is that our worship services are orchestrated to perpetuate this myth of American exceptionalism. Why else does the liturgy of Christianity adopt the liturgy of the nation-state? Why do Christians celebrate Thanksgiving Day, Mother's Day, Independence Day, or Memorial Day? These are not holidays (*holy days*) that belong to the narrative of Christianity; these days belong to the false soteriological narrative of the state. It is the state's means of ordering the year and teaching her citizens to remember her heroes, her stories, her families in order that the state can, through the spending of money that runs concomitant these holy days, continually renew itself. Some churches neglect Jesus' command to not swear oaths (Matt 5:34; Jas 5:12) and actually cite the pledge of allegiance during their services. How odd is it that followers of an executed criminal now make promises to his executor? This liturgy, with its own rituals and stories, has, despite the separation of church and state, not only merged with the story of Christianity but it has co-opted the story of Christianity. Such co-opting is dangerous as it becomes evident that Christianity no longer, if it ever did, narrates America. America tells the story of Christianity so Christians must understand their faith through the lens of America. I imagine this is why many sanctuaries are simply not complete without

7. For more on this and other stories engrained within this nation see Hughes, *Myths America Lives By*.

a cross and an American flag. I only wonder what would cause a bigger problem: the removal of the cross of the removal of the flag?

Theologian Lee Camp tells the story of his four-year-old daughter's end of the year preschool program that included the singing of various Christian songs.[8] One of those songs was the relatively popular, but none too lyrically challenging, "Our God is an Awesome God." The song was written by Rich Mullins and contains such lyrical wisdom as: "When He rolls up His sleeves He ain't just putting on the ritz, there is thunder in His footsteps and lightning in His fists." Truth be told the first time I heard this song (I lived a tortured teenage life), I thought he was talking about either Thor or Zeus. That actually interested me. It was not, however, the verse that became popular, but the chorus: "Our God is an awesome God / He reigns from heaven above / with wisdom, power, and love / our God is an awesome God." I have always found this popular song, originally geared toward children and teenagers but now to adults, to be problematic as it assumes this posture of animosity toward those who "have" a different God. It is sort of a glorified version of "my dad can beat up your dad." Camp realizes this when he states that what really made him nervous was the fact that these children just happened to be sporting t-shirts with American flags on them. Some of them were even waving their nation-state's flag in their tiny hands as they were singing about their God. It did not take Camp long to figure out that what was really being sung was "America's God is an awesome God."[9]

Such is the context that North American Christians interpret Scripture. We live in a post-Christian society yet desperately seeking to maintain some semblance of Christendom. A prime example of this runs rampant in campaign speeches. Despite the constitution's forbiddance of any merger of church and state, presidential candidates find it necessary to mawkishly parade their "private" faith commitments in order to secure the vote. "God Bless America" (apparently God has no choice in the matter) is uttered out of the mouths of ever governor, senator and official of this republic. It is simply mandatory if one is to survive in the world of politics. The United States is now, according to her leaders, the city on the hill that cannot be hidden (Matt 5:14) while busily soaking up two-thirds of all the world's resources in order to prove that God has indeed, even

8. Camp, *Mere Discipleship*, 144–45.
9. Ibid., 145.

at the expense of others, blessed us. We are told that God will continue blessing us as long as we continue to remember that God has chosen us to be God's messenger to the world. Once this is forgotten God's judgment, claims conservative Christianity, rains down on the United States as it once did the wandering Hebrews. Similar to those who blamed Rome's fall on those who institutionalized Christianity at the expense of the ancient Roman cults, Americans forgetting that it was founded on Christian principles (it was not, the so-called founding fathers were primarily deists) is, supposedly, leading to the collapse of the United States. Who is blamed every time a tragedy, whether it is terrorist attacks or hurricanes, strikes the sacred soil of America? It is either secularists, humanists, atheists or any other "non-patriotic" soul unwilling to prostrate themselves before the deity of the empire. To be a good American, for many within this culture, means that one must be a good Christian, and to be a good Christian one must be a good American. To challenge one is to implicitly challenge the other and it is for this reason that scripture has become such an important tool of American imperialism. It has become a tool used against the very ones who seek to be faithful to the God of all empires, not just the American one. The Berrigans, it is my contention, are a great bane to Christians in the United States primarily because their prophetic voice is bitter to those who so easily assume that their nation-building is on par with God's will.

A strong critique of the Berrigans often arises out of Paul's letter to the church in Rome. It is located in first two verses of chapter thirteen:

> Let every person be subject to the governing authorities; for there is no authority except from God, and those authorities that exist have been instituted by God. Therefore whoever resists authority resists what God has appointed, and those who resist will incur judgment. (Rom 13:1–2)

This is not the only passage used against Christian lawbreakers. A similar sentiment is found in 1 Pet 2:13: "For the Lord's sake accept the authority of every human institution, whether of the emperor as supreme, or of governors, as sent by him to punish those who do wrong and to praise those who do right." Both of these passages are very clear that Christians are to practice and teach subordination to the government. This includes all governments. While sitting in jail, under Nero no less, Paul demands that Christians are to be submissive to all powers that be because, despite how fallen they are, they are ordained by God. Rebellion against such powers is understood as rebellion against God. This is a chief line of defense from many within the Christian camps that insist that the questioning of a nation's laws is equivalent to questioning God. The Berrigans, it appears, are in disagreement with both Paul and Peter. This sort of thinking that is used against the witness of the Berrigans was also used against Martin Luther King, Jr., Clarence Jordan, the Catholic Worker, as well as the German Christian Dietrich Bonhoeffer who resisted Hitler and the National Socialists. Neither Paul nor Peter differentiates between which authorities Christians are to be subordinate to, their argument is that all powers are in place by God and, therefore, rebellion is sinful.

If this is truly the case then it makes little sense as to how such an argument can be taken seriously by Christians in the United States. The United States, after all, was founded on explicit disobedience to Scripture. It only comes into being as a result of its rebellion against the God-ordained powers of English monarchy. I fail to see how persuasive such an argument can be given that Christians have no problem rebelling against the English or celebrating such rebellion annually in July.

Nevertheless, this is a serious criticism and one that must be addressed in this Christ-haunted nation. I like Romans 13 as well as the chapter that precedes it. In Romans 12 Paul reminds Christians that we are a different kind of people. Our behavior must reflect the odd beliefs we entertain. He states that we must not "conform to this world" and proceeds to explain what that looks like:

> Bless those who persecute you; bless and do not curse them. . . . Live in harmony with one another; do not be haughty, but associate with the lowly; do not claim to be wiser than you are. Do not repay evil for evil . . . so far as it depends on you, live peaceably with all. Beloved, never avenge yourselves, but leave room for the wrath of God; for it is written, "Vengeance is mine, I will repay, says the Lord." No, "if your enemies are hungry, feed them; if they are thirsty, give them something to drink" . . . Do not be overcome by evil, but overcome evil with good.

I have yet to see any nation adopt this kind of thinking as a manifesto for its citizens and this is definitely not creedal for the world's greatest superpower.

I do not, however, think that just any nation should adopt this as a manifesto or creed. Such admonitions are not timeless principles that any person, regardless of their own particular narrative, can adopt and live by. Christianity does not function this way. This is a way of life for those people who have consciously adopted, and have been adopted by, the unusual path of Jesus. This is a path that demands love of enemies, turning the other cheek, the sharing and/or giving away of goods, and even subservience to those institutions that are directly at odds with such a way of life. This path is so radical it refuses to even resist those powers that would crucify its followers.

So there is a tension here. Christians are to refuse conformity with the world while being subservient to the very thing that often demands conformity to the world. How is this to be lived? If Peter claims one moment to not resist the authorities of this world, and then at another to "obey God rather than any human authority" (Acts 5:29), while Paul demands that we remain subordinate to the powers-that-be while refusing to be like them, then we must ask: How is this to be enacted? Part of the manner in which I have attempted to resolve or highlight this tension has been through the witness of certain Christian radicals of the twentieth century. It may, however, be erroneous to place such magnitude on this tension. Perhaps it is not so much a matter of balancing what appears to be different prescriptive guidance as much as it is the lens by which we read this scripture needs to be replaced.

In his book *Mere Discipleship*, Camp argues that Christians in the United States suffer from a peculiar ailment that he refers to as a Constantinian cataract.[10] By "Constantinian" he is calling attention to the upheaval that occurred with the conversion of the Roman Emperor Constantine. Though many historians cast doubt on the authenticity of his conversion, that he represents a major turning point in the history of Christianity cannot be denied. Under his reign Christianity not only enjoys toleration but eventually becomes the state religion. Christendom is born. The first three hundred years of Christianity enjoyed a period ripe with martyrdom, persecution, and the practice of nonviolence from its adherents. After Constantine, the persecution of Christians ceased but at the expense of the Christian's nonviolent witness. Just-war theory had to be developed in order to justify the Christians' engagement in war. Many adjustments were made, the chief among them being that Christians were now in charge. Prior to the beginning of the fourth century it was hardly

10. Camp, *Mere Discipleship*, 21–23.

imagined that Christians would find themselves in a position by which they would ever become like those gentiles who call themselves benefactors and lord their power over others (Matt 20:25–26). Yet, this did occur, and with it a new hermeneutic for reading Scripture. Though we now find ourselves in a post-Christendom age, much of how we read Scripture still assumes some level of power, some sense that we should be in charge dictating, for the good of all, what the world should be like. We assume Christians should be in charge and it is through this Constantinian lens that we continue to read scripture.

Read in this manner it is easy to see how Romans 13 becomes an apology for the status quo. Paul becomes a spokesperson for the acquiescence and buttressing of every movement of the government. Christianity, at best, becomes nothing more than a desperate competing principality and power trying to gain influence in order to regulate the behavior of both Christians and non-Christians.

This was surely not a practice of either Jesus or the early church. One cannot command faith. If so, why do Christians continue to treat their governments as the ultimate bearer of history? In terms of Romans 13 it is helpful to remember a few things, the first of which is that Paul spent a significant amount of time in jail while writing some of his epistles. If anything, that should provide us with some sort of indication as to how to read this passage. If we read him as one who does not upset the status quo or as one that is conformed to this world then he was clearly not following his own advice. His being in jail as well as his eventual execution demands that we rethink what he means when he tells us to be subordinate to power.

Secondly, Romans 13 is not the key text to understanding government in the New Testament. As John Howard Yoder reminds us, there is a strong strand of Gospel teaching that understands all nations as under the province of Satan.[11] In the gospels of Luke and Matthew Satan takes Jesus up to the top of a mountain "and showed in him in an instant all the kingdoms of the world. And the devil said to him, 'To you I will give their glory and authority; for it has been given over to me, and I will give it to anyone I please. If you then worship me, it will all be yours." (Luke 4:5–7;

11. Yoder, *The Politics of Jesus*, 194. Yoder provides a thorough exegetical account of Romans 13 and how it does not demand obedience but subservience. The difference between the two, for Yoder, is the difference between faithful and unfaithful Christian discipleship.

Matt 4:8–9).When Satan offers Jesus all the kingdoms in the world if Jesus would just worship him, Jesus does not refute Satan's claims of owner-ship. Jesus simply refuses the offer. His kingdom is not like any kingdoms of this earth. Yoder notes that many within our current democratic age find such an idea to be repulsive given that *we* are the government. For Christians under a modern democratic order to understand such a form of authority as Satanic is too much for our prideful ears. If Satan really is "prince of the air" (Eph 2:2) and does have the power to give control to those that bow to him, then all New Testament texts on governments must be read differently.

Finally, Paul was writing to Christians living under a pagan govern-ment. Though all forms of authority may, ultimately, be under the rule of God that a pagan body was in power runs counter to the notion of a providential ordering by God. Why would God purposely place nonbe-lievers in power? In order to kill God's faithful? Did God orchestra the placement of Nero and Diocletian in order to bear witness to the good-ness of God? Did God convince millions of Germans to place the most tyrannical leader in the twentieth century, Adolf Hitler, in office so that God's glory might be revealed to the world? Did God put in power the likes of Stalin, Pinochet, Reagan, Castro, and Bin-Laden? If so, could God not do a little better?

I do not intend to sound blasphemous, I am simply being mindful that the law, though ultimately ordained by God for the good of God's creation, is fallen. Just because a government is ordered by God does not mean that its actions are good. These powers are also subject to God and require the church, as God's bearer of God's message, to speak truth to power. Our present situation is even trickier as we live in a democratic order in which, at least theoretically, the people are the government. Yet what this entails is a realization that it is fallen creatures placing into positions of power other fallen creatures that attempt to enact a world according to a sinful and crooked vision of the good. Though as follow-ers of Jesus we must remain submissive to these powers they are not the highest good and, along with Peter, we must, when it comes to moments of choice, follow the law of God and not humans. Neither Peter nor Paul require that we practice unquestioned obedience to the powers-that-be, only that we are submissive to them. If any authority demands that we act in a manner antithetical to Christian discipleship then we must fol-low Jesus, not Caesar. The radical nature of Romans 13, following Paul's demands that we refuse conformity to the world, is that even under the most tyrannical of governments Christians are to obey Jesus and remain submissive to even the powers that crucified him.[12] It is not a matter of locating good governments for the Christian to bless and bad ones to condemn, but subordination to all governments *is* the Christian form of rebellion.[13] However, when governments demand that we burn their incense, that we eat their sacrificial meat, that we pledge oaths of loyalty to them then we must end up like the early Christians who chose to die on a stake rather than indulge their leaders' attempts at worship. If nothing else, we should at least end up like Paul, Daniel or Philip: sitting in prison writing letters to churches.

BABYLON'S BABY(LON)

"Shepherds? There is not one in the American Church! They are upper-management people for the most part. And they are the State's sheep!"

—PHILIP BERRIGAN

Once Christian faith is wedded to the state, it becomes sectarian. Christian faith is limited to the borders that are brutally defended by nation-states. The God of Christians is now a tribal god; a god only of one geographical locale. Rather than being a body of people whose faith knows no borders or boundaries, Christianity becomes fixed as a spatial boundary. It becomes limited to a certain time and space that can only grow inasmuch as the empire itself expands. The church is no longer catholic, she is no longer universal. The church, just like all nation-states, becomes sectarian by limiting its allegiance to that of her government's borders. Rather than being a body of people who endure through time and space, Christians set up camp in their respective nations and model a space based on the model of temporal authorities. In turn, North American Christianity, as a spatial entity, is not just situated within a Babylon, it *becomes* a Babylon. I

12. Yoder, *The Politics of Jesus*, 202–3. This is an interesting point of contention with the decision by the Berrigans to flee from the federal authorities for their crimes. Daniel Berrigan calls into question what he claims is a mythology at work in this country that makes a moral necessity out of assuming the consequences of breaking immoral laws. For more on their decision to not practice subordination see Polner and O'Grady, *Disarmed and Dangerous*, 218–32.

13. Ibid., 200, 209.

am suggesting that Christians in North America have found themselves, due to their own making, within a sort of double Babylonian captivity. Christianity, as a fixed space, is a Babylon within a Babylon desperately wanting to merge with that latter Babylon. This is a big problem for according to St. John, Babylon's future destruction is already determined (Rev 17–18).

During his exile to the island of Patmos, John began writing letters to various churches. These letters became known as the book of Revelation and have haunted, perplexed, and entertained Christians for two thousand years. I have to admit that as a child this particular book enabled me to survive many a boring sermon. It occasionally still does. Part of its great lure is its tendency to speak of creatures with multiple heads, dragons rising out of oceans, and cosmic battles between good and bad angels. On one extreme of the hermeneutical spectrum John appears to have suffered from the inhalation of toxic plants, for others it is the divinely-inspired outline of prophecy involving locusts, famines, as well as the occasional Pope, communist, and oil reservoir in the Middle East. I find both accounts unsatisfying as these polemical ends of the spectrum dismiss the kind of politic John attaches to Christianity. Whatever is being revealed in John's apocalypse appears to present a significant tension between the power of God and the powers of this world. This is not just the powers of the world that are not North American, but all powers of the world. Those who are tempted to easily mistake a close connection between earthly and heavenly powers may wish to take a close look at the book of Revelation. John depicts the nations of the world as predatory beasts demanding total allegiance of its citizens. He warns us that the giving of our allegiance to anything other than God is damning. The issue becomes particularly thorny when nation worship is conflated with God worship. What happens when Christians assume that the projects of their particular nations are aligned with the will of God? How careful must we been when our leaders inform us that every decision that our government makes is blessed/dictated by the God of all nations? One must be wary of the warning John gives us in chapter thirteen of Revelation:

> The beast was given a mouth uttering haughty and blasphemous words, and it was allowed to exercise authority for forty-two months. It opened its mouth to utter blasphemies against God, blaspheming his name and his dwelling, that is, those who dwell in heaven. (Rev 13:5–6)

Just in these two verses alone, the word blasphemy is mentioned three times. Blasphemy is often thought of in terms of taking God's name in vain. Due to this notion, cursing has posed a particular problem for the more pious traditions of Christianity in North America. Though it may be the case that obscenities mouthed by Christians are indeed sinful, John makes us painfully aware that blaspheming God is an affair that goes beyond mere "bad" words. I had the good fortune of being a teaching assistant to the now Methodist bishop of Alabama Will Willimon while he taught at Duke University. In one of his classes he told the story of a street preacher in South Carolina who enjoyed proving his faith via the handling of imaginary snakes. Willimon explained to us that this preacher never failed to end his sermons with the attempt to prove his apostolicity by telling his audience that if he only had a snake to hold they would see that he does indeed speak as God's messenger. According to Willimon, one day an old farm boy decided to take the preacher up on his offer. He waited until the right moment and just as the preacher claimed his desire for snakes to handle the young man threw two of them at the preacher. As the serpents landed on the preacher the preacher immediately screamed "God damn it!" quickly fleeing the scene. Willimon challenged us to discern how it was that the preacher was taking God's name in vain. Though it is easy to be offended by the language used by the preacher it is more difficult to understand how his claims of speaking for God are an abuse of God's name. The street preacher claimed God as the giver of his message. The farm boy tested the spirits and discovered that the truth was not in him.

I connect the story of the beast in Revelation to the street preacher in South Carolina because Christians in the U.S. face the danger of living with an established Christianity. Søren Kierkegaard claimed that the "apostasy from Christianity will not come about by everybody openly renouncing Christianity; no, but slyly, cunningly, by everybody assuming the name of being Christian."[14] The danger of Christianity as an established norm is that we all too easily assume our practices are God-ordained and, thus, beyond reproach. Like the street preacher, we fall prey to thinking that as long as we attend church and vote responsibly our paths are aligned with the path of God. But how often do our self-assured private and political practices betray an unwillingness to truly test the

14. Quoted in Camp's *Mere Discipleship*, 105.

spirits? How do we not know that we have been culturally inundated by a Christianity that is more American than Christian? This is where the Berrigans are so helpful. In a sense, they are like two snakes thrown at us. Their adamant protests reveal to us how many of our assumptions about what it means to be a Christian go unquestioned. Our empire informs us on a routine basis that its expansion into the world, its subsuming of other nations under the wing of the largest military superpower in history, is all part of God's will. God is, because we have claimed it, on our side. God blesses *only* America. Such a god can only be a god to other nations if other nations conform their politics to the politics of the United States. Given this reality, the bible no longer functions as a prophetic source that calls American practices into question. Instead, it is a tool used to ensure the riches of a nation that happily assumes its every desire is on par with God's will. But the Berrigans challenge all of this by their manner of protests. They purposely intend to shock us because they are shocked that Christians are so at peace with war. Their activities are meant to make us pause at how we have so easily refused to walk the path of nonviolence. This implicitly renders being a good and faithful citizen of the United States a problem. The United States, if it is to continue to function as it currently does, requires a strong military presence ready at any moment to defend, and extend, our right to pursue happiness. Yet, Jesus does not advocate for our rights—especially our right to be happy. Jesus calls us to servitude. This is a far cry from the indoctrination Christians receive by their nation's leaders. Though the first three centuries of Christians put away the sword it has made a strong come back. Sixteen hundred years later most Christians wield the sword (or at least endorse the wielding of the sword) with little to no hesitation. Just war theory has yet to deter the majority of Christian involvement in an American war. Its development only led to the adulteration of Jesus' simple but demanding message of love of enemy. From Christian nonviolence to just war theory, from the crusades to Christian realism, we have all too easily made peace with the most secular of instruments: the sword.[15] Though Jesus disarmed Peter, Christians have found a way to re-arm themselves. This is not an easy hermeneutic to overcome. It requires more than a re-reading of the Sermon on the Mount. It demands seeing such peaceable love in action. The Berrigan's actions were admittedly so extreme because they felt it

15. Berrigan, *Testimony: The Word Made Fresh*, 81.

necessary to wake American Christians up to their collusion in ongoing violence. They wanted Christians to remember that they follow the Prince of Peace, not a god of war.

It is interesting that Christians would need to be reminded that their God is not one of the Roman or Greek gods of war/bloodlust: Ares or Mars. We do, after all, live in a nation where many religious people adamantly desire the public display of the Ten Commandments. One of these commandments tells us not to kill but when you have a god more in line with Ares than Jesus, such prescriptions are easily maneuvered. We have claimed ownership of how scripture will talk to us. Since we have determined that scripture will be read in such a way as to not pose a threat to our insatiable bloodlust, we can no longer make sense of the Christ that has come and put an end to war itself. It is very difficult for North American Christians to imagine how Jesus' injunctions to not do harm, to refuse to retaliate, or to return evil for evil is more than allegorical attitude adjustments. It represents a posture that Christians are to embrace if they are to show the world who it is they claim to know. As Daniel writes, it is really quite simple:

> Christ will not shed the blood of another; He will only allow His own blood to be shed. Christ will not be complicit in murder. He will die, but He will not kill. And so the summons: We are not permitted to kill, or be complicit in killing. The prohibition stands firm: no matter the cause at issue, no matter the provocation, no matter the flags or polls, no matter the president, no matter the generals, the heavy triumphant faces and desert fatigues and flashpan victory. Every gun must fall from Christian hands, every missile must be transformed to a plowshare, every heart and structure must be disarmed. The attendants of the nonviolent Christ do not fight, kill or wage war.[16]

No matter how glorious out nation-state's media and filmmakers wish to convince us war and the sacrifices made in war are, Christians know that there are no acts of redemptive violence or redemptive sacrifices. Jesus suffered violence so that we could be saved from perpetrating it on others. That is our distinctive privilege to share with the world. It does not mean it will be easy. It is the way of Jesus and such costs must be considered as there is much to lose. There is also much to gain:

16. Ibid., 82.

Peacemaking is hard

hard almost as war.

The difference being one

we can stake life upon

and limb and thought and love.

I stake this poem out

dead man to dead stick

to tempt an Easter chance—

if faith may be

truth, an evil chance

penultimate at last,

not last. We are not lost.[17]

LOSING MY RELIGION

God didn't call America to engage in a senseless, unjust war . . . And we are crimi-
nals in that war. We've committed more war crimes almost than any nation in
the world, and I'm going to continue to say it. And we won't stop it because of our
pride and our arrogance as a nation. But God has a way of even putting nations
in their place . . .

—Martin Luther King, Jr.

After arresting Philip for a second time an FBI agent, who was also a
Catholic, said, "Him again? Good God, I'm changing my religion."[18] Here
were two Catholics attempting to be faithful to what they both held to
be true. The FBI agent was trying to enact justice. He was attempting to
uphold the law in such a way that left him without any recourse to how
such laws might conflict with his faith. On the opposite end was another
Catholic, a priest, forcing the agent to arrest him due to the his concern
to also enact justice. These two Catholics not only operated under opposing accounts of justice, but opposing accounts of Christianity. It was
a very truthful and telling comment the agent made when he suggested

17. Berrigan, *And the Risen Bread*, 100.
18. Berrigan, *Fighting the Lamb's War*, 96.

a possible change in his religion. For he was claiming that if this is what Christianity is all about, then he would need to look elsewhere. The federal agent understood quite well that the politics of his own faith were radically opposed to the politics of Berrigan's faith. Because of this difference, the agent was quite ready to abandon his religion it if required the kind of life lived by the priest. Such honesty is admirable and necessary for any faithful commitment to Christianity. It demands of us to state with the federal agent that it may be time for a change in our religion. For if both claim to be practitioners of the same faith, yet are clearly at odds with one another in form of life, then how do we know which is the more truthful mode of Christian performance: the arrestee or the arrested?

I imagine the manner in which I have posed this question is not entirely fair. It seems to suggest that there is no in-between, that Christianity is a matter of all or nothing, or that if you are not protesting war then you are not a Christian. This may be the case. The Berrigans think that Christian involvement in war is not possible. Therefore, any complicity in war marks a falling away from the Christian path. For them, the path of Jesus is totally encompassing and does not make for the kind of compromise by which Christians can claim to work in some sort of "in-between" status. In terms of governmental practices, Christians, according to the Berrigans, simply cannot support any republic that threatens or makes use of violence in order to secure its existence. The path of the Christian is at odds with the path of those seeking to *secure* the peace of the city rather than seeking its peace through the proclamation of the nonviolent witness of the peaceable kingdom. The path of the Christian is one in which the participant can only be a bearer of the truth. Such truth-telling demands that we be like Christ before Pilate whose next to last words was his declaration that he came into this world in order to bear witness to the truth. In his book *Testimony: The Word Made Fresh*, Daniel discusses how it is important, regardless of the consequences, to speak truth to power.[19] He reflects on John 18 where Jesus is being questioned by Pilate. Pilate asks Jesus if he really is the King of the Jews to which Jesus asks Pilate where his question originates. Pilate tells Jesus that he is only going by what Jesus' "own nation" (John 18:35) has said about him and then asks Jesus what he has done to anger so many people. Jesus answered,

19. Berrigan, *Testimony*, 80–82.

'My reign does not belong to this world. If my reign did belong to this world, my attendants would be fighting to keep me from being handed over to the Judeans. But as it is, my reign is not here.' So Pilate said to him, 'So you are a king?' Jesus answered, 'You say that I am a king. For this I was born, and for this I came into the world, to testify to the truth. Everyone who belongs to the truth listens to my voice.' (John 18:33–37)

Though Pilate offers those of Jesus' own nation an opportunity to free their king, the chief priests quickly inform Pilate that they have no other king but the emperor (John 19:16). Jesus is crucified by Roman power in collusion with the established religious piety of his own nation.

How easy it is to mimic those chief priests. The Berrigans show us how our actions betray the content of the claim, "We have no king but the emperor." Christian participation in an order that idolatrously claims to be the bearer of God's message, to be the city on the hill, a light to all nations providing freedom and democracy for the world is but another way of worshipping false gods. We have confused presidential concession of belief in God with the costly path of discipleship. We have deified our leaders in an attempt to deify ourselves. In a democracy our leaders are only but reflections of our own wants and desires. Desires to impose our wills, desire for power, and the desire to name what is God's will and what is not. We have not come very far at all from the days of Roman Caesars claiming divinity. In fact, we have come full circle.

Epilogue: Failing Faithfully

Perhaps the most insidious temptation to be avoided is one which is characteristic of the power structure itself: this fetishism of immediate visible results.

—THOMAS MERTON

The king was furious. Such display of rebellion could not go unpunished. To rebel against the law demanded retribution and the king delivered. The furnace was ordered seven times hotter than normal. It was so hot that the guards who cast Shadrach, Meshach, and Abednego into the furnace were immediately consumed by the flames. The three rebels, however, suffered no harm.

King Nebuchadnezzar, we are told, was astonished (Dan 3:24). He peered into the furnace only to grow more confused as he saw four men in the fire, all unbound walking around unharmed. He told them to come out. As the three walked out of the furnace (the fourth disappeared), the king proclaimed his amazement: "They disobeyed the king's command and yielded up their bodies rather than serve and worship any god except their own God" (3:28). Nebuchadnezzar passed an ordinance that any people or nation that blasphemed their God would be torn limb from limb and their homes would be laid to waste (3:29).

The king, like all kings, worshipped power. He chose their God because no other god exhibited such saving strength. Despite their allegiance beyond Babylon, he placed the three Hebrews in positions of authority. The king, for a moment, converted. Through the lives of these three who refused to obey the king, they showed him another way. They were not his "yes-men." They were not sycophants. By disobeying the king they did what was best for the king. Their "no" to the king was for the good of the king and his nation.

This narrative reminds us that even unjust rulers can be converted. In this particular case, a miracle truly happened. It is not just the young men that are saved, but their oppressor is also delivered. He is saved because of their refusal to worship his idols. They could have complied with the king's demand and decided that religion was a private matter and that oaths sworn to those in power are not problematic. Instead, they chose to obey God rather than the law of humans.

Unfortunately, the king does not fully understand that which has saved him. Shadrach, Meshach, and Abednego's worship of God is not based on potential reward. Their refusal to worship other gods was not predicated on the certainty that they would be saved as they admit to not knowing whether or not they would be rescued (3:18). Faith is not, as Daniel Berrigan reminds us, a "bargain struck in the market, no canny eye to a main chance. To say 'I believe' is to hand over to life and death (that is, to the God of life and death) a blank check."[1] The king, who eventually goes insane, worships their God because of what this god can do for him. The three young men worship God because only God is holy and worthy or worship.

In our utilitarian-driven culture the means are almost always justified by the ends. If something works, it is considered good. If something is efficient and produces tangible results, then it too is good. This sort of thinking infiltrated the life of Nebuchadnezzar as it continues to infiltrate all aspects of our lives. From war to marriage to religion, the ends justify the means. The murdering of hundreds of thousands of Japanese civilians in Hiroshima and Nagasaki was permitted and viewed as morally legitimate because it ended the war. Marriages are rarely viewed as coupled paths of discipleship accountable to the church but are ends in themselves justified only by the immediate sense of happiness one gains from it. Christianity in North America is justified and God is good *because* Christianity can make us wealthy, healthy, and successful. That it has become justified by its immediate results is the very thing that drives the omnipresent gospel of success movement characterized by the Osteens, Meyers, and Warrens.

This leaves us in a predicament when considering the witness of the Berrigans, Clarence Jordan, Dorothy Day, and Peter Maurin. On their journey toward the city of God one of the many things that they shared in common was failure. Very few African-Americans actually joined *Koinonia*, Maurin's farm communes hardly took off, Day wondered if they

1. Berrigan, *Daniel: Under the Siege of the Divine*, 63–64.

were making even the slightest dent in poverty, and the Berrigans' actions did little to halt or even shorten the war in Vietnam (or, later, Iraq). When discussing these people it is inevitability pointed out to me, including the students in my classes, that their way of life has not brought poverty, racism, or war to an end. Therefore, what justifies their lives? Philip Berrigan spent much of his life in jail separate from his wife and children, and "for what?" protests my students. His actions, the assumption is made, are worthless because they produced so few tangible results. The Berrigans, I am told, are a failure. Sure, the Catholic Worker and *Koinonia* may have helped a few people along the way, but at the end of the day is this not a sign that all of their hard work should have been directed elsewhere? Does not their inability to produce considerable results prove the futility of their tactics? If so, does this not discredit the kind of God they claim to worship? Who would worship a God whose followers consistently fail, or at least do not affect any real change in society? Surely this is not the God that so ardently blesses the good people of the American Empire with material gain and geographical conquest?

If not, who is the God that these people reflect? It could be the God of Jeremiah who wept at the prospect of his mission. It could also be the God of John the Baptist whose head ended up on a silver platter. Paul was belittled by those who claimed to be the true apostles of God, and Jesus was forsaken by his followers (and, according to him, his Father) at his crucifixion. The first three centuries of Christianity saw little change in the habits of the pagan empire and Christians paid the price of death for their convictions. Given this record, perhaps the argument can be made that the inability to affect "real" change or develop a large group of followers is more in line with the prophets of Israel and the apostles of the early church? Based on the track record of the vast majority of Israel's prophets and the demise of the majority of Christ's disciples' it may be the case that failure is a sign that one is bearing witness to the path of Jesus. When did success ever become the litmus test for revealing the one who told us not to expect better treatment than him? I am not arguing that failure is an unconditional sign of God's kingdom, only that truth is not determined by consensus. These Christians should not be written off as unfaithful if their lives do not produce so-called results. Their inability to be accepted by many within the empire's mainstream religion may be a sign that they are in this world, but not of it.

Very few of the Hebrew prophets are known for their success stories. Their mission comprised of having to utter the difficult words "Thus saith the Lord . . ." followed by hostility and accusations that the speaker was a liar. For this reason, "successful" ministers, pastors and evangelists should make us a little nervous. This is not to suggest that God's Word must of necessity fall on deaf ears, but in a rebellious creation any time large numbers of people do respond, as in the case of ministries ranging from Billy Graham to Joel Osteen, we may do well to check the content of the message. Are we being asked to conform to the way of Christ or the way of the world? I have yet to discover the immediate attractiveness of an order predicated on the execution of a criminal. Jesus taught, lived, and demanded jubilee, servitude, nonresistance, and the kind of forgiveness that extends to violent enemies. This just does not seem to parallel the presentation of the Gospel in our culture of profiteering, imperial expansion, hostility toward immigrants, and pride over the ability to squash enemies. Yet, more so than ever, Jesus remains popular. I imagine this popularity is due primarily to our ability to see Jesus as the chief architect of the American empire. When it comes to what we think is good, beautiful and true, Jesus mirrors us. It is very easy to love the one created in our image.

POOR PROFITS/PROPHETS

In this world, history continues not because of what kings and presidents might do but because ravens keep alive a prophet starving in the desert (I Kings 17) and because even as kings and presidents count their people and take their polls and plan the future, the word of God comes into the wilderness (Luke 3).

—DAVID TOOLE

In the sixth chapter of Isaiah the prophet hears God ask, "Whom shall I send, and who will go for us?" Isaiah quickly responds, "Here am I; send me!" This verse has become well known due to Dan Schutte's popular song "Here I am Lord." Though many enthusiastically sing this song during their worship services, it is the latter part of the passage that seems to go ignored. Isaiah's excitement at being a prophet of God is curtailed when he realizes that his message is destined for failure. Isaiah assumes the task but is told that the message he will bear will not be understood.

Isaiah's own people will listen, but they will not comprehend (Isa 6:9). Isaiah asks how long such misunderstanding will occur. God responds, "Until cities lie waste without inhabitant, and houses without people, and the land is utterly desolate . . ." (Isa 6:11). It is only then, in the smallest manner, by the tenth of the people that may survive God's judgment, will the holiness of God's kingdom be understood. The prophet Isaiah is commanded to give a message that will go unheeded. This is by no means an exception in Israel's history of prophets; it often appears to be the norm. That this norm is assumed by the apostles and those that journey in this tradition should not be surprising. To bear witness to the truth in a rebellious world rarely ends as a success story.

Of course, there are the Jonah's. There are those who speak the truth, even begrudgingly, and entire cities convert and are saved. There is Nathan, who speaks truth to King David, and David repents. There is the story of Shadrach, Meshach and Abednego: three youths whose brief appearance in scripture is legendary because they resisted the law of the land and led its king into the depths of madness. Neither failure nor success can be the ultimate assessment for faithfulness. Perhaps the examination of only the results is to peer in the wrong direction. We must ask questions regarding whether or not our witness is in line with the Gospel while realizing that how we read the Gospel is already, in part, determined by our current habits and practices. This is difficult as we cannot always discern how we have been shaped to read scripture prior to even reading it.

One thing that can help, I believe, is to respond with charity and hospitality to the Christians within this book. By this I mean we must ask the question, "What if they are right?"[2] What if Peter Maurin and Dorothy Day were right to say that the coat in our closets belong to the poor? What if Clarence Jordan was right to say that the biggest lie told in America is that Jesus is Lord?[3] What if the Berrigans were right about the necessity of Christians placing their bodies between weapons and other humans? Such charity may lead us to take seriously their path of prophetic Christian anarchism.

---

2. This is the way Lawrence Cunningham in his *The Catholic Heritage*, phrases the issue in regards to what may be considered the "fanatical" activism of the Berrigan brothers (182–83).

3. Lee, *Cotton Patch Evidence*, 225.

That the reactions of our twentieth-century Christian activists may seem so extreme is due to their closeness to Israel's prophets. The prophets were driven almost beyond the borders of sanity when they witnessed the injustices perpetrated by their own people. The Rabbi Abraham Joshua Heschel reminds us that what might be to us a slight injustice, something like cheating in business, is to the prophets a disaster: "To us injustice is injurious to the welfare of the people; to the prophets it is a deathblow to existence; to us, an episode; to them a catastrophe, a threat to the world."[4] The Days, Berrigans and Jordans of our time recognize these catastrophes. They understand how it threatens the existence of God's creatures.

A DIFFERENT MODE OF BEING

Every perfect life is a parable invented by God.

—Simone Weil

The German anarchist Gustav Landauer once remarked, "The state is not something which can be destroyed by revolution, but is a condition, a certain relationship between human beings, a mode of human behavior; we destroy it by contracting other relationships, by behaving differently."[5] Throughout this book I have never argued for the destruction of the state, but only for the creation and sustaining of alternative forms of being in this world that reflect the politics of Jesus. I have attempted to do this via not so much theoretical argument, but by the lives of a few Christians in the twentieth century who refused to be defined by the world's understanding of politics. By examining the Catholic Worker, the *Koinonians*, and the Berrigans, I have tried to highlight a certain antipathy that this fallen world has toward the poor, those of different races, and how nations name and react toward their enemies. All three groups responded, at times differently, yet they all retained a certain form of life congruent with one another. They pressed for the sharing of goods, they lived in intentional communities, and they practiced nonviolence. All of these Christian anarchists attempted to exemplify this notion of constructing different modes of behavior, different relationships, and a different condition of being. They understood that to be Christian was to be different.

4. Heschel, *The Prophets*, 4.
5. Ward, *Anarchy in Action*, 9.

They were different from the world, from the secularists, from the pious, they were different from the capitalists and they were different from the communists. Even though they lived in a manner that might best be described as anarchical, they were different even from the anarchists. The difference resides in their conviction that a Jew from Galilee was raised from the dead in order that God's creation might know God. They wanted to share in his resurrection, and they wanted to share in it while they were still alive. For it is in Jesus' resurrection that we find hope in the midst of Babylon.

Bibliography

Aquinas, Thomas. *Summa Theologica* II–II. Translated by the Father of the English Domincian Province. Notre Dame, IN: Christian Classics, 1981.

Augustine. *Concerning The City of God Against the Pagans.* Translated by Henry Bettenson. London: Penguin, 1984.

Bakunin, Mikhail. *God and The State.* New York: Dover, 1970.

Bernasconi, Robert & Lott, Tommy L. *The Idea of Race.* Indianapolis, IN: Hackett, 2000.

Bernasconi, Robert. "Who Invented the Concept of Race? Kant's Role in the Enlightenment Construction of Race" *Philosopher Annual.* 24 (2003) 11–36.

Berrigan, Daniel. *And the Risen Bread: Selected and New Poems 1957–1997.* New York: Fordham University Press, 1998.

———. *Testimony: The Word Made Fresh.* Maryknoll, NY: Orbis, 2004.

———. *Daniel: Under the Siege of the Divine.* Farmington, PA: Plough, 1998.

Berrigan, Philip. *Fighting the Lamb's War: Skirmishes with the American Empire.* Monroe: Common Courage, 1996.

Berry, Wendell. *The Hidden Wound.* New York: North Star, 1989.

Bonhoeffer, Dietrich. *The Cost of Discipleship.* New York: Macmillan, 1969.

Breitman, George. Ed. *Malcolm X Speaks.* New York: Grove, 1990.

Brook, Wes Howard and Anthony Gwyther. *Unveiling Empire: Reading Revelation Then and Now.* Maryknoll, NY: Orbis, 1999.

Camp, Lee. *Mere Discipleship: Radical Christianity in a Rebellious World.* Grand Rapids: Brazos, 2003.

Cavanaugh, William T. *Theopolitical Imagination: Discovering the Liturgy as Political Act in an Age of Global Consumerism.* London: T. & T. Clark, 2002.

Celano, Thomas. Translated by Placid Hermann, O.F.M. *St. Francis of Assisi.* Chicago: Franciscan Herald Press, 1988.

Chernus, Ira. *American Nonviolence: The History of an Idea.* Maryknoll, NY: Orbis, 2004.

Chrysostom, John. *On Wealth and Poverty.* Translated by Catharine P. Roth. Crestwood, NY: St. Vladimir's Seminary Press, 1999.

Clark, Stephen R. L. *The Political Animal: Biology, Ethics and Politics.* London. Routledge, 1999.

Cone, James. *Martin and Malcolm and America: A Dream or a Nightmare.* Maryknoll, NY: Orbis, 2000.

———. *God of the Oppressed.* Maryknoll, NY: Orbis, 2001.

Cullman, Oscar. *The State in the New Testament*. New York: Scribners, 1956.

Cunningham, Lawrence. *The Catholic Heritage*. Eugene, OR: Wipf & Stock, 2002.

Dark, David. *Everyday Apocalypse: The Sacred Revealed in Radiohead, The Simpsons and Other Pop Icons*. Grand Rapids: Brazos, 2002.

Day, Dorothy. *The Long Loneliness: The Autobiography of Dorothy Day*. New York: HarperCollins, 1997.

Day, Dorothy, and Francis J. Sicius. *Peter Maurin: Apostle to the World*. Maryknoll, NY: Orbis, 2004.

Dear, John. *You Will Be My Witnesses: Saints, Prophets and Martyrs*. Maryknoll, NY: Orbis, 2006.

Eller, Vernard. *Christian Anarchy: Jesus' Primacy over the Powers*. Eugene, OR: Wipf & Stock, 1999.

Ellis, Marc. *Peter Maurin: Prophet in the Twentieth Century*. New York: Paulist, 1981.

Ellsberg, Robert. *All Saints: Daily Reflections on Saints, Prophets, and Witnesses for our Time*. New York: Crossroad, 2000.

Ellul, Jacques, *Anarchy and Christianity*. Translated by Geoffrey W. Bromiley. Grand Rapids: Eerdmans, 1991.

Eusebius, *The History of the Church from Christ to Constantine*. Translated by G. A. Williamson. London: Penguin, 1985.

Goldberg, David Theo. *The Racial State*. Oxford: Blackwell, 2002.

Guerin, Daniel. *Anarchism*. New York: Monthly Review, 1970.

———. *No Gods, No Masters: An Anthology of Anarchism*. San Francisco: AK, 1998.

Hauerwas, Stanley and Wells, Samuel. Ed.s *The Blackwell Companion to Christian Ethics*. Oxford: Blackwell, 2004.

Hauerwas, Stanley and William Willimon. *Resident Aliens*. Nashville: Abingdon, 1989.

Heschel, Abraham Joshua. *The Prophets: An Introduction*. New York: Harper, 1962.

Horowitz, Irving Louis, Editor. *The Anarchists*. New Brunswick, NJ: Aldine Transaction, 2005.

Howell, James C. *Servants, Misfits, and Martyrs: Saints and their Stories*. Nashville: Upper Room, 2000.

Hughes, Richard. *Myths America Lives By*. Chicago: University of Illinois Press, 2003.

Inchausti, Robert. *Subversive Orthodoxy: Outlaws, Revolutionaries, and Other Christians in Disguise*. Grand Rapids: Brazos, 2005.

Johnson, Kelly. *The Fear of Beggars: Stewardship and Poverty in Christian Ethics*. Grand Rapids: Eerdmans, 2007.

Jordan, Clarence. *The Cotton Patch Version of Paul's Epistles*. New York: Association, 1968.

Kafka, Franz. *The Blue Octavo Notebooks*. Cambridge: Exact Change, 1991.

Krimerman, Leonard I, and Lewis Perry, editors. *Patterns of Anarchy*. Garden City, NY: Anchor, 1966.

Lee, Dallas. *Cotton Patch Evidence*. New York: Harper & Row, 1971.

Lewis, Alan. *Between Cross and Resurrection: A Theology of Holy Saturday*. Grand Rapids: Eerdmans, 2001.

Long, D. Stephen. *Divine Economy: Theology and the Market*. London: Routledge, 2000.

―――. *The Goodness of God: Theology, The Church, and Social Order*. Grand Rapids: Brazos, 2001.

Long, Michael. *Against Us, But For Us*. Macon, GA: Mercer University Press, 2002.

Marsh, Charles. *The Beloved Community: How Faith Shapes Social Justice, from the Civil Rights Movement to Today*. New York: Basic Books, 2005.

Maurin, Peter. *Easy Essays*. Chicago: Franciscan Herald, 1984.

McClendon, James Wm. *Biography as Theology: How Life's Stories Can Remake Theology*. Philadelphia: Trinity, 1990.

Milbank, John. *Theology and Social Theory: Beyond Secular Reason*. Oxford: Blackwell, 1991.

O'Donovan, Oliver. *The Desire of the Nations: Rediscovering the Roots of Political Theology*. Cambridge: Cambridge University Press, 1996.

O'Donovan, Oliver, and Joan Lockwood O' Donovan, editors. *From Irenaeus to Grotius: A Sourcebook in Christian Political Thought 100–1625*. Grand Rapids: Eerdmans, 1999.

Paolucci, Henry, editor. *The Political Writings of St. Augustine*. Washington DC: Regenery Gateway, 1962.

Polner, Murray and O'Grady, Jim. *Disarmed and Dangerous: The Radical Lives and Times of Daniel and Philip Berrigan*. New York: Basic Books, 1997.

Proudhon, P. J. *What is Property? An Inquiry into The Principle of Right and of Government*. New York: Howard Fertig, 1966.

Rassmusson, Arne, *The Church as Polis? From Political Theology to Theological Politics as Exemplified by Jürgen Moltmann and Stanly Hauerwas*. Notre Dame, IN: University of Notre Dame Press, 1996.

Read, Herbert. *Anarchy and Order*. Boston: Beacon, 1971.

Roberts, Alexander and James Donaldson, Editors. *Ante-Nicene Fathers*. Vol. I. Peabody, IL: Hendrickson, 1999.

―――. *Ante-Nicene Fathers*. Vol. III. Peabody, IL: Hendrickson, 1999.

Snider, P. Joel. *The "Cotton Patch" Gospel: The Proclamation of Clarence Jordan*. Lanham, MD: University Press of America, 1985.

Stringfellow, William. *An Ethic for Christians and Other Aliens in a Strange Land*. Eugene, OR: Wipf and Stock, 2004.

―――. *Conscience and Obedience: The Politics of Romans 13 and Revelation 13 in Light of the Second Coming*. Waco, TX: Word, 1977.

Trocme, Andre. *Jesus and The Nonviolent Revolution*. Maryknoll, NY: Orbis, 2004.

Veysey, Laurence. *The Communal Experience: Anarchist and Mystical Communities in Twentieth Century America*. Chicago: University of Chicago Press, 1978.

Wallis, Jim and Joyce Hollyday, Editors. *Cloud of Witnesses*. Maryknoll, NY: Orbis, 2006.

Ward, Colin. *Anarchy in Action*. London: Freedom, 1988.

Ward, Graham. "Why is the City so Important for Christian Theology?" *Cross Currents* 52:4 (2003) 462–73.

West, Cornel. *Prophesy Deliverance! An Afro-American Revolutionary Christianity.* Philadelphia: Westminster, 1982.

Wilson, Catherine, Editor. *Civilization and Oppression.* Calgary, Canada: University of Calgary Press, 1999.

Wink, Walter. *Naming the Powers: The Language of Power in the New Testament.* Philadelphia: Fortress, 1984.

———. *The Powers That Be.* New York: Double Day, 1998.

Woodcock, George. Ed., *The Anarchist Reader.* New York: Harvesters/Humanities, 1977.

X, Malcolm. *The Autobiography of Malcolm X.* New York: Ballantine, 1983.

Yoder, John Howard. "Armaments and Eschatology," *Studies in Christian Ethics* 1:1 (1988) 43–61.

———. *For the Nations: Essays Evangelical and Public.* Grand Rapids: Eerdmans, 1997.

———. *Nevertheless: Varieties of Religious Pacifism.* Scottdale, PA: Herald, 1992.

———. *The Christian Witness to the State.* Eugene, OR: Wipf & Stock, 1998.

———. *The Politics of Jesus: Vicit Agnus Noster.* Grand Rapids: Eerdmans, 1994.

———. *The Priestly Kingdom: Social Ethics as Gospel.* Notre Dame, IN: University of Notre Dame Press, 1984.

York, Tripp. "Dethroning a King." *Christian Ethics Today* 14:1 (2008).

———. *The Purple Crown: The Politics of Martyrdom.* Scottdale, PA: Herald, 2007.

Index

Abednego, xi–xii, 103–4, 107
Adam, Karl, 42
allegiance, xiii, xvi– xvii, 16, 19, 20,
   22, 25, 31; 94–95; Christian 5;
   heavenly 4; pledge of 87
Ambrose, Saint, 49
Amish, 39
Amos, xii, xvi, 65
Anabaptist, 14; intentional communities
   75
anarcho-capitalist, 37n
anarcho-communist, 8
anarchical posture, xiii, xiv, 5, 37n
anarchy, anarchism, xiii, xv, 1, 5–14, 40,
   79; Christian 15–16, 30, 107
anarchist, 6,–12, 15, 27, 37–38, 41,
   48–49, 108–9 Christian xiv, xv, 1,
   13–14, 82; pacifist 10n; politic xiv,
   16; secular 14; societies 5
Anti-Imperialist League, 42
anti-political, 10, 28–29
apocalyptic, 13, 23, 27, 80; language 25;
   order 26; people 26; politic(s) xiv,
   16, 25–26
apocalypticism, 16
Aristotle, 12n
Aryan Nation, 64
Azaraiah, xi
Augustine, Saint, 17, 34, 42, 82
autonomy, 12, 54–55

Babylon, xi, 24–25, 33, 80, 94–95, 103,
   109
Bad Religion, 86
Bakunin, Mikhail, 11, 37, 48
Ballou, Adin, 14
baptism, xv–xvii, 14, 18, 69, 74; post- 3
baptismal practices, xvii

Batterham, Foster, 41
beatification, 35
Berdyaev, Nicholas, 13–16
Berkman, Alexander, 11
Bernardone, Giovanni di, 53–54
Beecher, Henry Ward, 5
Bernasconi, Robert, 62n
Berrigan, Daniel, xiii, 34, 81–86, 89, 90,
   94, 97–98, 99n, 100–101, 104–5,
   107–8
Berrigan, Philip, xiii, xv, 34, 81–86,
   89–90, 94, 97, 99, 100–101, 104–5,
   107–8
Berry, Wendell, 37, 70–71
Bohemian Brethren, 14
Bonhoeffer, Dietrich, 34, 35, 90
Breitman, George, 67–68n
Brook, Howard Wes, 24n
Bruderhof, 39
Buddhism, 18n
Burns, Dan, 25n

Caesar, 14–15, 20, 22, 25, 32, 93, 101
Camp, Lee, 33, 88, 91, 96n
capitalism, 37–40, 54, 59
Carter, Kameron J., 61
Catholic Worker Movement, xvi, 11, 39,
   44–47, 59
Catonsville Nine, 84
Cavanaugh, William, T. 2
Chelcicky, Peter, 14
Chernus, Ira, 10n
Christ, xiii, xvi, 2, 4, 11, 13–14, 20n,
   21–23, 26–27, 32, 35, 42, 46, 58,
   73–75, 86, 90, 98, 100, 105–6 see
   also Jesus
Christendom, 54, 88, 91–92

Church, xiii, xiv, xv, xvii, 2, 6, 11, 14, 17, 18, 19, 20, 21, 22–28,30, 33–36, 38, 40–42 46–47, 50–51, 55–56, 70–71, 73–76, 82–83, 87–89, 92–96

citizenship, xiii, xvii, xiv, 18–21, 35, 61

civil disobedience, xvii

civil rights, 64, 65, 67, 68, 69, 75, 78

Clark, Stephen R. L.,12n

clergy, xvii

common good, 47–48, 54

communism, 1, 40, 76

Cone, James, 68, 69n

Constantine, 91–92

Constantinople, 44, 49

constitutionalist, 6

creation, xi, 4n, 13, 17, 20–21, 24–25, 37, 46–47, 72, 80, 93, 109

crucifixion, xv, 13, 26, 105

Cullman, Oscar, 30n

Cunningham, Lawrence, 107n

Damascus, 26

Daniel, xi, xii

Dante, 38–39

Dark, David, 26n

Day, Dorothy, xiii, 11, 15, 28, 34, 40–46, 49–52, 55, 59, 104, 107, 108

Dear, John, 85n

democracy, xiii, 1–2, 10, 12, 79, 101

democrat, 4, 6, 22

Diaspora, 34

discipleship, xi, xiii, xiv, 10, 34–35, 47–48, 72, 78, 92n, 93,101, 104

Doerge, Halden, x, 13n

Domination System, 30

Eberhard, Arnold, 39

Eberhardt, David, 83

economy, 38–39 46, 51, 57, of God 35; of the triune God 17; divine 35

Eller, Vernard, 10n, 29–30

Ellis, Marc, 43n,

Ellsberg, Robert, 41n

Ellul, Jacques, 10n

England, Martin and Mabel, 74

English Diggers, 14

epistemology, 17, 45

eschatology, 27, 80

Esther, xii

Eucharist, Eucharistic, 14, 44

Eusebius, 20n

exile, 4–5, 20, 24, 33–34, 36, 95

faith, 2, 3, 7, 40–42, 74, 87, 92, 94, 96, 99–100, 104

fellowship, 73, 75

Foucault, Michael, 29

Francis, Saint, 34, 42, 51, 54–56

free choice, 12

freedom, 1, 10–17, 25, 40, 49, 55, 60, 62, 64–66, 68, 101

Fuller, Millard and Linda, 77

God, xi–xvii, 1, 3, 4–6, 10–11, 14, 17, 19–27, 31, 33–36, 40–41, 47–58, 73, 75, 82, 85–91, 93–99, 101, 103–9; command of 60; justice of 2; kingdom of 2, 28, 29, 69, 74, 76, 80; people of 32, 81; Son of 30, 72

Goldberg, David Theo, 61

Goldman, Emma, 11, 13

Gospel, gospel, 28, 83, 92, 104, 106–7

Graham, Billy, 106

Gwyther, Anthony, 24

government, 5–8, 10–13, 20, 48–49, 78–80, 84, 89, 92–95; practices 100; property 82

greed, 38–39, 53; economic xvi

Guerin, Daniel, 7n, 9n, 11n

Guevera, Che, 30

Hale, Matthew, 64

Hall, Gordon, 67

Hamer, Fanny Lou, 60, 68, 80

Hammerskins, 64

Hannaniah, xi

Havel, Vaclav, 28–29

Hauerwas, Stanley, 17n, 22, 46n

heaven, xiv, 18–21, 25, 58, 88, 95

Hebrew, Hebrews, 58, 67n, 89, 103, 106

Hennacy, Ammon, 11

Heschel, Rabbi Abraham Joshua, 108

Hollyday, Joyce, 70n

Horowitz, Irving Louis, 7n, 8n
Hosea, xii, 65
Howell, James C., 58n
Hughes, Richard, 87
Hume, David, 12
Hutterites, 39

idolatry, xii, 2, 19, 101, 104; anti- 87
imperial seduction, 24
imperialism, 15, 89
incarnation, xvii, 30
injustice, xvi, 16, 78, 108
Inchausti, Robert, 27–29
individualism, 12
inner self, 12
integration, 65–66
Islam, 18n, 68
Israel, xi, 4, 21, 50, 87, 105, 107–8

Jehovah's Witnesses, 19n
Jeremiah, xii, 4, 32–34, 105
Jerusalem, 24–25, 34–35
Jesus, xii, xiv, xv, xvii, 3, 6, 7n, 13–16,
     21–23, 26–27, 29–35, 38–41,
     46–47, 51, 53, 55, 57–58, 71–75,
     79, 82, 84, 86–87, 91–94, 97–98,
     100–101, 105–9 *see also* Christ
Jewish, Jews, xi, 4, 24, 33–34, 73–74, 82,
     87, 100, 109
Joan of Arc, 34
John, Saint, 23–25, 42, 95–96
John Chrysostom, Saint, 49, 58–59
Johnson, Kelly, 53, 57
Jonah, 33, 107
Jordan, Clarence, xiii, 15, 34, 69–81, 83,
     90, 104, 107–8
Judaism, 2, 18n, 38
justice, xvi, xvii, 2, 4, 26, 57, 60, 64–65,
     69n, 81, 99; social 72
just-war theory, 91, 97

Kafka, Franz, 25
Kant, Immanuel, 62–63
Kierkegaard, Soren, 1, 96
King Jr., Martin Luther, xv–xvi, 28,
     64–65, 67–69, 73, 78, 83, 90, 99
Koinonia, 74n, 75–78, 104–5, 108

Krimerman, Leonard I., 8n, 11n, 14n,
     16n
Kropotkin, Peter, 8, 13, 37

Lamb, the, xiv, 22–23, 26–27
Landauer, Gustav, 108
Larrimore, Mark, 63n
Le Sillion, 43
Lee, Dallas, 76n, 107n
Lewis, Tom, 83
liberalism, 11–13, 65, 68
Locke, John, 12, 65n
Long, D. Stephen, 38n, 64–65, 66n
Long, Michael, xi
Lott, Tommy L., 62n

Malatesta, Errico, 7–8
Malcolm X, 65–69, 73, 80
     Mantz, Felix, 34
Marsh, Charles, 75, 78
martyr, 5n, 20, 81–82
Martyr, Justin, 19
martyrdom, 20, 48, 91
Mary, xiii
Masons, 19n
Maurin, Peter, 34, 42, 43n, 45n–47n, 49,
     51–53, 54n, 55, 56n, 104, 107
material, materialism, xvi, 38, 59, 75, 83;
     blessings 51; gain 52, 105
McClendon, James, 71n
Mengel, Rev. James, 83, 84n
Merton, Thomas, 28, 103
Meshach, xi–xiii, 103–4, 107
Milbank, John, 35–36
militarism, xvi, 40, 75, 83, 85–86
Mishael, xi
missiology, xiii, 4, 17
monarchy, 1, 3, 6, 31, 90

National Socialists, 90
nation-state, 2–3, 5, 7, 9, 12–13, 21, 24,
     31, 60–61, 87–88, 94, 98
natural order, 8
Necessity Defense, 85
Ninevites, 33
Nebuchadnezzar, xi–xii, 103–4
Nietzsche, Friedrich, 27

Nero, 89, 93
nonviolence, xvi, 10, 32, 44, 47, 65, 72, 91, 97–98, 100, 108

Origen, 19
orthodoxy, 14
O'Donovan, Joan Lockwood, 19
O'Donovan, Oliver, 4n, 19
O'Grady, Jim, 94n
O'Toole, David, 23, 106
Osteen, Joel, 104, 106

Paolucci, Henry, 82n
Paul, Saint, xiii, 20–21, 26, 31, 52, 74, 89–94, 105
Perry, Lewis, 8, 11, 14, 16
Peter, Saint, xiii, 20–21, 35, 52, 90–91, 93, 97
Plowshares Eight, 84
Plowshares Movement, 81
politic, xiv; anarchist 16, 21–23, 27, 30, 35, 48, 61, 95–97; Christian 16; of Caesar 14; socio- 37
political ideology, xiii, 1, 4, 12–14
political theory, 1, 10–13
politics, xiv, xvii 2, 18, 21–23, 27, 28–30, 47, 60–61, 65, 68, 88, 100; Christian 10; of Jesus 108; of money 39; Roman xv
Polner, Murray, 94n
post-baptism, 3
poverty, 40–41, 48, 52–54, 57–59, 67–68, 71–73, 78, 84, 105
Propagandhi, xi
Proudhon, Pierre-Joseph, 6–7, 11n, 13, 37–38, 48–49

racism, xvi, 60–66, 68–73, 75, 78, 80, 83–84
rebellion, 23, 29, 31, 35, 90, 94, 103, 106–7
redemption, 14, 17, 21, 24–25, 31, 80, 98
Read, Herbert, 5
republican, 4, 6, 22
resurrection, xiv–xv, 13, 26–27, 109
Revelation, 24, 95–96

revolution, xvi, 1, 29–31, 108; green 44; personalist 44
Rome, 20–21, 24, 26, 36, 89
Rousseau, Jean-Jacques, 12
Ruth, xii

salvation, xv, 1–2, 24, 27, 46, 51, 55
salvific language, 2
Sanctus, 20n
Sarah, xii
Satan, 2, 29, 67n, 92–93
Schutte, Dan, 106
segregation, 66–68, 78
separation, 66–67
Shadrach, xi–xiii, 103–4, 107
Sicius, Francis J., 42n–43n
Simon the Zealot, 30
slavery, 15, 25, 48, 64–66, 73
Snider, Joel P., 72n
socialism, xiii, xvi, 1, 40, 67n
socialist, 1, 48
society, 8–9, 14, 35, 56, 64, 105; anarchist 6; Christian 19; non-materialistic 59; political 19; post-Christian 88
soteriology, 2, 31, 47, 87
stewardship, 17, 75
Stringfellow, William, 13, 24–25

Teresa of Avila, Saint, 42
Tertullian, 17, 19–20, 34
theocracies, 1
Thessalonians, 31
Thibon, Gustave, 53
Thomas Aquinas, Saint, 49n–50
Thomas of Celano, 53–54
Tolstoy, Leo, 14
triple axis of evil, xv–xvi
Trocme, Andre, 30n
True Levellers, 14
Truth, Sojourner, 80
tyranny, 4, 13–15, 27, 54, 65, 93–94

usury, 38–39

Veysey, Laurence, 14n
Volin, 9

Waldensians, 14
Ward, Colin, 108n
Ward, Graham, 35
Wallis, Jim, 70n
Weil, Simon, 108
Wells, Samuel, 46n
West, Cornel, 61–65
Willimon, William, 22, 96
Wink, Walter, 30–31, 32n
witness, xiii, xiv, xv, xvi, 3–4, 13, 15,
    17–18, 21–23, 27–28, 33–34, 36,
    39–40, 55, 59–60, 68–69, 72, 75,
    77, 79–80, 90–91, 93, 100, 104–5,
    107–8
Woodcock, George, 8n
World Church of the Creator
    Movement, 64

Yoder, John Howard, 4n, 10n, 17, 26,
    30n, 33–34, 92–93, 94n
York, Tripp, 5n, 33n, 46n

Zinn, Howard, 5
Zizek, Slavoj, 77

Made in the USA
San Bernardino, CA
21 January 2017